MW00566027

THIS BOOK WILL TEACH YOU

CAREER SUCCESS

THE INSIDER'S GUIDE
TO MAKING THE MOST
OF YOUR CAREER

This book may be ordered by mail from the publisher. Please include $5.99 for
postage and handling. Please support your local bookseller first!

Books published by Whalen Book Works are available at special discounts
when purchased in bulk. For more information, please email us at
info@whalenbookworks.com.

Whalen Book Works
68 North Street
Kennebunkport, ME 04046

www.whalenbookworks.com

Printed in China
1 2 3 4 5 6 7 8 9 0

First Edition

"TO FIND A CAREER TO WHICH YOU ARE ADAPTED BY NATURE, AND THEN TO WORK HARD AT IT, IS ABOUT AS NEAR TO A FORMULA FOR SUCCESS AND HAPPINESS AS THE WORLD PROVIDES."

—MARK SULLIVAN

CONTENTS

INTRODUCTION

This Book Will Teach You Career Success is a guide for those who are starting new jobs after college, or who have been out of the game for a while and want to take the next step forward! Whether you're working for a Fortune 500 company, a financial firm, a small start-up, an activist nonprofit, or a local small business, you'll no doubt have hopes and goals about where your career can take you. Thankfully, these tips and techniques for career success can be applied to almost any situation and any job!

In this useful guide, you'll learn about the psychology of success and what it takes to get in the right frame of mind to go for it! You'll read about networking and how helping others helps you, and the importance of building solid relationships that will be long-lasting. Most importantly, you'll learn how to define and set goals for yourself that you can achieve! If you're not sure about what to do next in your career, if you know you could achieve more and give back more, but don't know how to make it happen, don't let those uncertainties and doubts stop you. *This Book Will Teach You Career Success* answers your questions and gives you a starting point to pursue and achieve those goals, with solid advice to make it happen.

The book is divided into chapters arranged by subject matter. Each offers you important information and gives you places to start working from. It won't give advice for your specific industry, but instead offers information that you can apply in any work environment, with an emphasis on how to succeed by also giving back. This book is a handy reference and guide for when you need to check on something about a specific topic. You may already know some of this information, whereas other information may be new to you. Read it in whatever order you wish, and feel free to dip into the text wherever is helpful to you. Each chapter (and each section) can stand alone but also holds together to give you a bigger picture.

A book of this size can offer brief summaries of each subject, but take in this information and use it to launch into further research and education. The Resources section at the end gives you a lot of helpful further reading, as well as useful websites that can give you far more information—especially concerning legal issues—than a small book can. Bear in mind that this book is not to be seen as a substitute for legal or any other kind of official advice. If you need further information on any of the subjects covered here, please investigate them on your own, using the Resources section as a starting point. Getting your career to where you want it doesn't have to be overwhelming and confusing. By using the tips and suggestions in this book, you can help further your own goals and get started on the path to the successful career that you want!

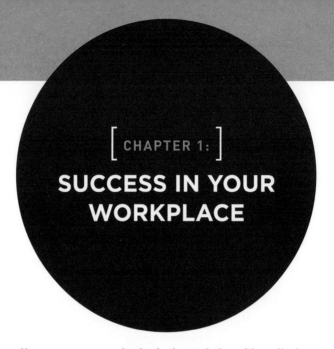

CHAPTER 1:

SUCCESS IN YOUR WORKPLACE

Your career success begins in the workplace; it's really that simple. The attitudes you adopt, the choices you make, and the actions you take at work will be the biggest indicator of how you progress and, ultimately, succeed in your career. Interestingly, a "career" can mean many things in the current work environment. People may change careers several times throughout their lives. The old practice of staying with a company for one's entire working life has become something of a relic of the past. These days, you're far more likely to change companies or even industries more than once, and that's fine. You can bring your experience and skills with you to new environments, and the same techniques for success should serve you well across multiple workplaces and even industries. This chapter gives you an introduction to some of the basics of working toward success at your job, wherever you are in your career and whatever you do.

THE PSYCHOLOGY OF SUCCESS AT WORK: EIGHT STRATEGIES

How you think about your work is as important as how you do it. Being able to go in with a successful frame of mind will give you a great advantage in setting and achieving goals, and in attaining job and career satisfaction. Adopting the right mindset about your career can help you to be ready for success. Here are some methods that you can use to cultivate a success-oriented way of thinking.

1. **Make it all about your attitude.** It goes without saying that how you approach your work will make a big difference as to whether you enjoy it and get the most out of it. When you start a new job, you may be excited, and the novelty will carry you for a while. But after a few months, a routine might set in, and you might find the polish is wearing off a bit. This is completely normal, so you'll need to create new ways to continue to make your job interesting and challenging. Maintaining a good outlook on your work is something that others will see and will be a good reflection on you in the long run.

2. **Make good first impressions.** From your first day on the job to months or even years in, you'll always be meeting new people. It's important to make sure those meetings leave a good feeling on both sides. Being professional, respectful, and courteous will always serve you well. The old cliché about never getting a second chance to make a first impression holds true. If someone doesn't view you as favorable from the

first time they meet you, it's going to be more of a challenge to work well with them in the future, much less ask for help if you need it later on.

3. **Make good second impressions.** Just as important as making your first meeting count, you need to be able to follow it up by creating the same kind of professional mood every time you interact with someone, especially if it's someone who could be of use to your advancement later on. You'll have your good days and bad days, just like everyone else; the secret is to make sure that even on your bad days, you bring your best to your job. If you're really struggling, talk to your boss if you are experiencing personal problems that could affect your work performance (see page 142).

4. **Be committed.** Obviously, you need dedication to your job; it's why you were hired. Consistently being able to come in with enthusiasm (even if you're not always feeling it), will be very helpful. You'll build trust with your coworkers and boss, and might even get the reputation as the go-to person for certain jobs. Being reliable helps others and yourself.

5. **Be helpful.** Always be willing to lend a helping hand. Your willingness to reach out and assist others is a great marker of your commitment to the company's success, and your own. The more you create a feeling of mutual assistance, the more likely someone will be willing to help you out when you get stuck, which will happen at some point.

6. **Think outside the box.** With any luck, your company will encourage independent thinking and problem-solving, and be pleased if you take the initiative on projects. Your commitment to doing that bit of extra work and trying to see issues from a different angle will likely be noticed by those higher up. If your

company discourages this kind of behavior, or if you find your boss or team leader micromanaging things too much, you may have consider whether this job is a good fit for you, and just how far you'll be able to advance in a confining environment.

7. **Set goals.** Set long-term and short-term goals for yourself, and be committed to seeing them through; see pages 14–16 for advice on how to do this.

8. **Learn from your mistakes.** Not everything is going to work out, not everything is going to go the way you want it to, and sometimes you'll just screw up. It's OK, it happens, and learning to accept this will help you a lot in the long term. Don't view mistakes as insurmountable disasters; use them as learning experiences, and make the commitment to try harder to prevent them in the future. Everyone messes up from time to time, so try to let it go, as much as you can.

> **"Act as if what you do makes a difference. It does."**
>
> **—WILLIAM JAMES**

SIX WAYS TO CREATE YOUR WORK PERSONA

We're always told to be yourself, and this holds true at work. We want to be in an environment where we are comfortable and can, indeed, be ourselves. But at the same time, it's important to consider how you present yourself on the job. You're taking on a new role that is different from your personal life, and this requires some adjustments. If you're starting work out of college, there will be a definite shift from what you're used to. Here are some suggestions for how to present as a professional and still be you.

1. **Start with what you have.** You are already a developed, well-rounded person, so you don't need to start over and change who you are. Regardless of your background, you've already undoubtedly been in many situations where professional behavior was called for, so use those as your guide. Be aware that you don't need to fundamentally change who you are or how you act. Think about those aspects of your personality that are absolutely essential to who you are and stick with those while crafting a work identity.

2. **Identify what's important to you.** What are your core values? What are the things you most want to achieve? Even if you are just starting your career, you probably already have longer-term goals in mind. Make a list of what they are and estimate when you would like to achieve them.

3. **Dress to impress.** Dress codes vary widely from business to business, and it's crucial that you get a sense of what you can and cannot wear. It's not a bad idea to overdress a little, especially right at the start of a job, but it's **always** a bad idea to underdress. A law firm will expect something very different from a tech company where the programmers sit in beanbags, so it's very important to understand the code before you even start work.

4. **Survey your office culture.** Get a sense of how others act in your workplace and look for ways to fit in. What is the general tone? Again, this doesn't mean that you have to fundamentally alter who you are, but you will need to get a sense of what kinds of behavior are expected. Is your boss fine with being addressed on a first-name basis, or is it "Mr." or "Ms."? If your office is very casual, then it's fine to go along with that, but if there is more formality, you'll need to adjust accordingly. You can still be you; you'll just have to be you in an appropriate way.

5. **Be invaluable.** One way to really identify yourself to your boss and coworkers is to be exemplary in your work. Meet deadlines, exceed expectations, and be seen as someone who goes above and beyond. This will become a part of your persona and help you stand out. If your goal is advancement with your company, you need to be noticed, and developing a persona of excellence is a great way to do it.

6. **Act professionally.** Whatever the tone of your workplace is, always be professional and courteous to others. It's fine to have fun and joke around at appropriate times, but treating others with respect is expected and vital to shaping a persona that fits in well at your job. You never want to be seen as the slacker, the goof-off, the one who's unreliable, or, worse, annoying or offensive.

SEVEN METHODS OF SETTING AND ATTAINING GOALS

A major part of your success will come from defining, setting, and working toward your goals. These don't have to be huge, career-shifting activities. You can start small and slow, and build up over time. Breaking bigger goals down into smaller parts makes them much more manageable. But even so, you can fall behind, or you can just skip them one week, and then make excuses as to why something didn't get done. If the idea of goal-setting seems daunting, even in small doses, here is some advice for making the work easier to do and keep up with.

1. **Take the time to understand each of your goals.** What is this goal, and what is its ultimate aim? Why do you want to achieve it? What conditions are you setting on it? When do you need to have it accomplished? If that doesn't happen, what is your backup plan? You need to have these kinds of questions and more in mind, whether for your own plans or for those you've been assigned by your workplace. How do your personal goals align with those of the company? Are they in harmony? Are they at odds? If the latter, is this a big problem, or is it something that can be reconciled? If you find that increasingly your own goals are at odds with your company's, it may be time to consider moving on.

2. **Get into specifics.** It does you no good to say, "Someday I'd like to . . ." You need details! Define exactly what your goals are and write down what you will need to do to accomplish them. You may not have all the information at first, but try to be as specific as you can. This goes for both short-term and long-term goals. If you need to get something done in two weeks' time, get clear on how you're going to do that. Create a plan, a timetable, or whatever works for you. You'll need to be able to monitor your progress, even day by day, if necessary.

3. **Keep things realistic.** You may be tempted to go all in on some goals and that's fine, but try to keep things in perspective. What can you realistically do in the time frame that you've established for yourself? Do you have the knowledge, the skills, and the means to accomplish what you want to do? Will you need outside help? It's fine if that's the case, but get clear about what assistance you think you'll need, and whom you might approach about obtaining it. Getting halfway into a project only to find that it can't be finished by you alone will be frustrating and set you back. Accept when you can't do something on your own and be open to help.

4. **Keep a regular schedule.** It does no good to make a plan and then chip away at it little by little when you feel like it, when you can spare a few minutes, or when you remember to do it. Once you have a well-defined goal and a plan to execute it, you'll have to discipline yourself to keep at it. The best way to do this is to break bigger tasks down into manageable smaller ones and try to do something every day. Plan out your tasks a week (or more) in advance. The more you get used to getting things done daily and on time, the easier it will be. Don't try to finish it all at once, and don't worry about not doing enough. Slow and steady really can win the race if you stay committed.

5. **Keep track of your accomplishments.** It's very important to check off things as you get them done, and even give yourself a little pat on the back for doing so. It will also let you see how far you've come and how much farther you still have to go. If you can see that you've done, for example, half of the work so far and on time, you have a great marker for your progress, and a little psychological boost. Take the small victories and let them add up to bigger ones. This practice will also help keep you from overdoing it. You don't want to risk spending too much time on one goal or project while neglecting your other work and other goals. Keep your work regular and measurable.

6. **Be ready for the unexpected.** You'll get offtrack, things will come up, you'll need to set aside your plans, you'll have to postpone something, and your best-laid plans will suddenly seem to be going hopelessly to blazes. And you know what? That's OK. Problems come up all the time, and it's entirely probable that sometimes your master plan will have to deal with some hiccups. Expect them, and if you can, even build a little extra time into your goal outline as a buffer. You may need to spend a few extra hours or days fixing up something that you didn't anticipate, but look at it as a way to learn more about what you're doing. And if your goal can't survive the occasional problem, it might need some reworking anyway.

7. **Monitor your progress.** This step is absolutely essential! Not only will it make you accountable, but also it will let you see how it's all coming along. Do this on a regular basis, whether every few days, once a week, or whatever seems best. For long-term goals, you may be able to check in once a month, but for anything more short term, a weekly update with yourself is probably a good idea. This is also a great way to practice keeping up with whatever you need to do to see your goals through. It's easy to say to yourself that you didn't get it all done this week, yet there's always next week, but if you check in with your progress and see exactly what worked and what didn't, you'll get more in the habit of not letting things slide. If you make a plan, you need to stick with it, and check-ins will force you to do that until it becomes a habit.

INTRODUCTIONS ARE EASY! (SOMETIMES)

From your first days and throughout your career, you'll be meeting new people. If you're working for a large company, you'll probably continue meeting people well after your first few weeks. You'll meet people at conferences and other professional gatherings, you'll meet them at business functions and dinners, and there may be some among them whom you really want to get to know and stay connected with. That's a lot of people! Fortunately, introductions are indeed fairly easy and, with a bit of practice, you'll be able to navigate them just fine.

- **The standard greeting is still the best.**
Simply make eye contact, smile, and shake their hand. A simple phrase such as "Mary, I'm Kate, nice to meet you!" is all you need. It's always good to repeat the person's name back to them, since this will help you remember it better.

- **Ask questions.** If you have the time to chat a little, ask the person a bit about themselves, what they do, etc. You don't need to retain all of the information (and honestly you probably won't), but it gives you both something to talk about to prevent awkward silences. If this is someone you've wanted to meet, this is a great chance to tell them something you admire about

them and ask them more about their work. Getting people to talk about themselves is a great way to keep a conversation going and build trust.

- **Mind your body language.** One way to make a bad first impression is to send signals that you are blocked off and defensive. Actions like crossing your arms, slouching, or putting your hands in your pockets can all come off as too casual or even rude. Listen, smile, nod, pay attention, stand (or sit) up straight, and respect the other person's space. **Never** interrupt or talk over someone!

- **Trade contact information.** Whether this is someone in another department or another company, it's always good to commit to staying in touch. Business cards are still the standard and reliable way to do this, especially for people higher up in your company or outside of it. But if the person is a peer at your workplace, even jotting down your email or number on a piece of paper can do the trick.

- **Follow up.** This is the important part. It does no good to go out and meet people if nothing ever comes of it. A short follow-up email thanking them for their time will do wonders. Now you've made a connection and opened a door. Be sure to keep it open by checking in with them periodically.

- **Don't hesitate to reach out.** If there is someone you want to meet at your workplace or elsewhere, it's fine to take the initiative and politely reach out to them.

- **Make use of your company's employee list.** Many companies have a roster of employees, which makes it easy for you to get in touch with anyone you want to.

- **Always be willing to meet others.** Believe it or not, other people may reach out to you, so always be willing to take a minute or two to talk, answer questions, and more. You might be surprised that you're getting a reputation as someone to know, someone whom others seek out. That's a great compliment and shows that you're doing the right thing. Keep it up!

[
"If it scares you, it might be a good thing to try."

—SETH GODIN
]

SEVEN WAYS TO CULTIVATE A GOOD WORKING RELATIONSHIP WITH YOUR COWORKERS

To be successful at your job and in general in your career, it's going to be essential to get along with your coworkers. While this may seem quite obvious, it may sometimes prove to be easier said than done. It's likely that you enjoy working with some people more than others, and maybe even find it a struggle to get along with some individuals. The thing is, you don't need to be best friends with everyone (and as they're your coworkers and not personal friends, it's better to keep some distance anyway). But you should be able to be cordial and professional with everyone. Here are some suggestions to keep everything going smoothly.

1. **Be on time and ready to work.** The simple act of being on time and ready to start the day is a great way of showing your colleagues that you care about the work and them. It really is as simple as giving them the same respect that you'd want in return.

2. **Be ready to contribute.** Speak up and offer your ideas in the spirit of collaboration. You obviously have the skills, so be sure to say your

piece. On the other side, be open to changing your views and approach; someone may see something that you don't. Listen and always consider other points of view. The idea is to cultivate a back-and-forth relationship with your coworkers that values everyone.

3. Invite others out. Your coworkers don't have to be your best friends, but they are people, and spending a little time away from the office can be a great chance to bond. Anything from lunch to an afternoon coffee to after-hour drinks can give you all a chance to relax a bit. Making these kinds of connections will let your time at work flow better as well. Take the initiative and extend some invitations from time to time, whether to just one other person or to a small group.

4. Accept other's invites. Equally important, make the effort to accept invites from your coworkers. You may not always feel like going out somewhere, and you're not obligated to do so every time, but if you consistently turn down offers, you're going to get a reputation as being standoffish and difficult to get to know, which is the last thing you want! Make the effort to tag along, at least some of the time.

5. Be a part of all team communications. Whatever your group's preference for staying in touch: emails, Slack or some other chat, or meetings, make sure that you stay up-to-date and in the loop with conversations. You don't want to be in the position of missing out and having to get caught up quickly, or, even worse, needing to have a coworker catch you up. On the other hand, be wary of chat time that gets out of hand. If you're expected to constantly keep up with messages even when you're off work, there may be a problem that needs to be addressed.

6. **Move around, if you can.** You may be working in an environment that doesn't bother with dedicated work spaces, and you're more free to choose where you want to work. If so, this is a great opportunity to move around a bit from day to day and get to know others better. It also may be a great chance to bounce ideas off new people and to offer your help to different people throughout the week.

7. **Bring your personality to work.** Obviously, you're there to do the job, but you've spent a lifetime being you and developing that, so make sure you let it out for others to see, at least a little. This may be nothing more than personalizing your work area a little (if you have one) and seeing if others have done the same. There is almost always something to converse about with these kinds of setups. Even just taking  a minute or two out of your time for a friendly chat will foster a better working relationship. Being authentic rather than trying to fit into some preconceived notion of who you should be on the job will serve you far better in the long run. Let your colleagues know that you're approachable, interesting, and even fun!

> **"Coming together is a beginning; keeping together is progress; working together is success."**
>
> **—HENRY FORD**

FIVE TIPS TO CULTIVATE A GOOD WORKING RELATIONSHIP WITH YOUR BOSS

An important part of having a successful career is being able to get on well with your superiors. If there are tensions and conflicts with your boss, it's going to make it harder for you to do your job, much less deliver the kinds of work that you want to in order to advance. Everyone fears getting stuck with a boss they hate, but often it just involves working through any snags. Here are some important things to keep in mind when working with a potentially troublesome boss.

1. **Each boss is only human, and they're all different.** No two bosses will be the same, and you'll have to adapt to their individual management style whenever you start at a new company or a new position. Never try to compare them, or you'll just end up being frustrated.

2. **Send the message that you're committed.** Be on time to work, obey the dress code and other codes of conduct, treat everyone with respect, and make the effort to do your job well. This all sounds very easy, but not being a problem employee will go a long way toward you being viewed favorably. Always be willing to contribute and go a bit farther. Be enthusiastic and take your work seriously. If you see problems and you know how they can be solved, take some

initiative and get to work on them. Many bosses like employees that don't need to be told to do everything.

3. **Take some time to get to know them.** This doesn't mean you need to become best drinking buddies (a very bad idea, incidentally), but getting a sense of who they are always makes for an easier working relationship. Your boss may come along on the occasional happy hour or other employee outing. Welcome them and be willing to sit and chat about things other than work. Creating a sense of comfort and ease in the off time will help make the working time that much smoother.

4. **Take the time to understand their management style.** Some bosses like to be very involved (maybe too much so!), while others will take a more hands-off approach. You may have a style that you prefer, but you'll have to be willing to adapt somewhat to their style. They may even tell you how they like to work right at the start. If not, observe how they act, and maybe even bring it up with your coworkers. The better you know how they operate, the more you'll be able to fit in and work well.

5. **Be careful not to take things personally.** Well, not right away. There could be any number of reasons why you and your boss are having friction. This uncertainty will be more likely when you are starting a new job or a new boss has come into your workplace. Maybe they're just having a bad day, maybe there's a personal problem, or maybe there really is an issue between you. Always remember to step back and not make any hasty decisions. If the conflict continues or recurs, you'll need to arrange to meet with your boss to try to talk things through. This will probably not be pleasant for either of you, but it will be necessary to ensure that things don't get worse.

SIX WAYS OF BEING A TEAM PLAYER WHILE ALSO FINDING YOUR OWN VOICE

In a traditional office environment, you'll be working together with many other people, who will come from different backgrounds, have different views and ways of doing things, and yet you all will need to work together to achieve the company's goals as well as your own personal aims. Being on a team can be exciting and inspiring, but it's important that you also bring your own individuality to the process: you were hired for your skills and expertise, after all! Here are some thoughts on retaining your identity in the crowd, and using that to further your own success.

1. **Own your space.** You're on this team for a reason, so own that and be proud of it. Everybody there is a part of the group because they bring something special and vital to the project. Get used to the idea that this includes you. You have as much right to be there as anyone, and your unique talents are a part of the reason why you're there. Together, all of you, as individuals, will work toward being greater as a whole.

2. **Understand your place.** This is especially true if you are the new person joining an established group. They may be completely welcoming, but they may not. If you're finding some resistance to your ideas or even your presence, you might need to be

patient until you've integrated into the group a little more and worked on projects together. If there is no room for your particular brand of working, you might ask your boss if there are other projects that you can work on alone as a creative outlet. And you may have to face the uncomfortable fact that this is not the place for you, especially if you don't feel valued or respected.

3. Identify what it is that you bring. Get clear in your own mind what value you are bringing to the team. What makes you unique? What skills and knowledge do you have that the others don't? Having a good sense of your own strengths will boost your confidence and help you be a better team member. At the same time, recognize others' strengths and what they do that you don't.

4. Be honest. Speak your mind about the way the process is going. If you're bothered by something, speak up. Don't be timid. You are a part of the team and, in theory, everyone's opinions should matter equally. If something is not working or you can see a better way of doing it, say so. You are entitled to bring both good and bad news. Don't just go along with the herd if there is something that is genuinely concerning you.

5. Address conflicts early on. If any problems do arise, don't let them go. They will only become bigger as time goes on, and be harder to solve. If you have a conflict with another team member over anything, try to arrange a time to talk it through. This can be one-on-one or with your boss present (or another mediator)—whatever is most comfortable to you.

6. Set your own boundaries. You need to be available to work on projects, but you cannot neglect your own life. If you need the weekend free for your own personal business or just to recharge, don't hesitate to inform others that you will be unavailable. You don't need to go along with groupthink that insists you owe all your time to the team or the company. If you find that too often your work is bleeding over into evenings or weekends, it may be time to say something, to your boss if not to the team itself. Taking time for yourself is never wrong. For much more on setting boundaries and looking after yourself, see *This Book Will Teach You to Own Your Time*, also in this series.

> **"The most difficult thing is the decision to act, the rest is merely tenacity. The fears are paper tigers. You can do anything you decide to do. You can act to change and control your life; and the procedure, the process is its own reward."**
>
> **—AMELIA EARHART**

A JOB VERSUS A CAREER: WHICH ONE DO YOU WANT?

Jobs and careers can be the same, or they can be very different. Many jobs are only stepping-stones to better things, and understanding where you are on those stones is important. A career can be made up of many jobs along the way, or you might decide to stay with one. How do you know if your current work is what you want to continue doing or if it's not so suitable for the long term? Here are some ideas about identifying your situation.

- **Ask yourself what you want your career to be.**
The most obvious place to start is to get clear about what it is you want to be doing. The old question "What do you want to be when you grow up?" still has relevance as an adult. The difference is that now we may make several full career changes throughout our lives, whereas our parents or grandparents may have stayed at one company their whole lives. With all of the changes in the economic situation over the past few decades, job security is less of a sure thing than it used to be. Also, more and more people want to explore other options as they age. They may leave the office world entirely and try something new. For now, ask yourself what you want for yourself over the next few years, and always be open to the fact that you may change your mind.

- **Review your long-term goals.** What do you want for yourself in terms of finances, job satisfaction, responsibilities, and related work topics by this time next year? How about in five years? Do you see yourself as moving up in your current company? Or are you thinking that you will need to jump ship and go elsewhere to meet your goals? Start mapping out some of your longer-term plans, so that you can create targets to meet. If you feel that there is only so far that your current job can take you, there's nothing wrong with planning on exiting from it in twelve months, or however long you feel you need.

- **What skills do you need?** What don't know you know now that you will need to know to advance? This could be anything from software or hardware to gaining additional qualifications and degrees. If you know that you will need more training and new skills, start making a list of what you'll need and how to go about obtaining them. The sooner you get clear in your mind the education you'll require, the better you'll be able to acquire it.

- **Are you advancing?** What's actually happening with your current job? Is there room for advancement, or are you starting to feel stuck? Do you keep being given vague promises of promotions, but they never actually happen? You'll need to look at your situation and get a sense of how you think you're doing in the company as a whole. If you're putting in a lot of work, going above and beyond, but still not impressing the higher-ups, it may be time to consider if your talents could be better used elsewhere.

Your career might involve several jobs over the course of your life. As you grow and learn more, you may move from one job to the next while advancing your overall career. You may even jump industries and do a related job, but not exactly the same as your previous work. This can still be considered part of the same overall career.

TEN LONG-TERM STRATEGIES FOR WORKPLACE SUCCESS

When thinking about your career success, the key word is "career," and you'll need to be looking at the long term as well as what you can do immediately. Even if you're relatively new to the work environment, it's a good idea to formulate some bigger goals and keep in mind where you want to go. If you're not sure if this is the industry for you, you can still make up some general plans that can be adapted later on. Here are some important things to keep in mind.

1. **Decide if this is your job or your career.** Honestly, it may be too early for you to know the answer to this question, but if you've been at the job for a year or two, or more, you probably have some sense about whether you want to stay in this industry or even at your current company. Knowing this will help you to make better and clearer longer-range plans.

2. **Keep tabs on your industry.** If you're interested in the industry (with or without your current company), keep up-to-date with what's happening in it. Read up on trends and predictions for what the next few years hold. Is it going to continue to grow? Is a downturn possible? Of course, we can never know for certain; some industries do well, while others sink, even if they were predicted to thrive. But having some sense of your industry's probable future will help you to sharpen your own vision for yourself.

3. **Make shorter-term goals.** Plan ahead for what you'd like to be doing in three months, six months, a year. What skills can you pick up those time periods? What projects do you want to be a part of? What can you do to ensure a great performance review? Anything that is related to your more immediate success will pay off for your bigger goals.

4. **Make longer-term goals.** And of course, make plans for the more distant future. These will of necessity be a little less precise, but they can be helpful signposts to keep you on your path. Having an idea of where you want to be in five years will give you the chance to break down the path to it into doable pieces that will seem more manageable.

5. **Develop action plans to implement your goals.** Just making lists of goals won't get you anywhere. For each goal, you need to have a plan. Make the effort to go into as much detail as you can. The more you can see from the outset what you need to do, the easier it will be to actually take action on them. If your goal is to learn a new software program, break it down into how much per day you need to devote to studying. Will ten minutes a day be enough? Fifteen? If you're committed to increasing sales by 20 percent by the end of the year, what exactly will you need to do to make this happen?

6. **Seek out important networking opportunities.** Keep an eye out for movers and shakers at your company and in your industry. The more important and influential people you know, the better. You may get the chance to help them out with something at some point, and it's likely they won't forget that.

7. **Work on skills of all kinds.** Make another list of everything you think you'll need to learn to advance in the way you want to. This can be anything from proprietary software, to certifications, to even just improving your phone skills or your ability to introduce yourself. Indeed,

so-called soft skills are kind of all the rage now, and include things that aren't just in a textbook, such as problem-solving, communication, managing your time, conflict resolution, empathy, and so on. Several other books in this series go into more detail about these kinds of skills.

8. **Advertise yourself.** Make sure you're known for what you do. This doesn't mean you need a neon sign shouting for people to look at you, but when you do well, be OK with taking credit for it. Offer your help frequently and with sincerity; let others come to see you as not only an expert at what you do but also as a stellar person who's great to work with and be around.

9. **Stick to the plan.** Once you've defined your goals, make your plans and follow them; it's a simple as that. Hold yourself accountable and make sure that you complete objectives by the deadlines you've set for yourself. It's good to have a trusted friend, colleague, or even family member in on this to keep you honest and on track.

10. **But also be able to adapt.** Things change, unforeseen circumstances arise, plans get screwed up. Don't be so set on your timeline or your plan of action that you refuse to see alternatives. Often, a new way of doing things is exactly what you need. Sometimes your best-laid plans will get derailed. There will be setbacks; there will be disappointments. But always keep an open mind and adapt to change, even if you don't like it. The branch that can bend in the wind will survive, but the one that's too rigid might break. Don't break.

PROMOTIONS AND RAISES

If you're career-minded, of course you're going to be thinking about your advancement possibilities at your company, and that includes these wonderful things: promotions and raises! But what if you feel you're not being recognized for your time and hard work? You may think that you deserve a raise, but how do you bring this up with your boss? You may feel uncomfortable, or like you're being demanding and unreasonable, or fear that you'll at least be seen this way? What if your boss says no? What if they fire you (unlikely, but still)? Here are some suggestions for how to prepare yourself to make your case and ensure your own advancement.

- **Arrange a meeting with your boss to discuss your situation.** During the meeting, reinforce your worth to the company, emphasizing your skills and contributions. Be careful not to compare yourself to your coworkers, because you may not know what their salaries are; some may be making less than you! This information is considered private if it's not volunteered, so don't go asking others what they make. What you can do is research the going rate for your kind of work in the industry to get some idea of whether you're making less or about the same as everyone else. That will give you a good starting point.

- **You may not get as much as you'd hoped for, or anything at all.** In this case, it's essential not to get angry or argumentative. There may be any number of reasons for this that have nothing to do with your value. The company may be on a strict budget at the moment and unable to accommodate you, even if it would like to. There may be no positions to fill that can accommodate you, or your boss just may not think you're ready. A no is unlikely to be personal, unless you have a history of confrontation with your boss or coworkers, so don't make it personal on your side. You'll just look unprofessional and possibly ruin your chances in the future.

- **You may get a counteroffer.** You may receive an offer for less than you wanted or for a job you hadn't thought of. They may also offer some additional benefits instead of as much money. In this case, you'll have to consider the situation. If the company budget just won't allow for them to give you as much as you'd like, can they give you an incremental increase? Maybe part now and more in six months' time? See if there is room for negotiation here. Maybe they can offer you some extra perks, like more flextime or the ability to work from home a few days a week. Saving money on your commute might add up pretty quickly and make up for the lesser raise they're offering. Maybe they'll throw in some more paid time off or extra vacation days. Maybe you can get a better working space or a new company computer. Look for ways that you can be compensated beyond just money.

- **If they say you're not ready.** Maybe you feel like you deserve a promotion, but your boss disagrees. Maybe your higher-ups think you're not quite ready yet for the extra responsibility. This answer can sting, especially if you've been working hard and feel you've earned it, but instead of getting angry, try asking what you need to do to be ready. Is there extra education or training you need? Would your company be willing to provide that to help you get up to speed? If they can see your potential and willingness to work with them to get to where they think you need to be, it may go a long way toward helping you eventually to attain that goal. Trust that others can sometimes see us better than we see ourselves, and that our wants sometimes get in the way of us being objective. Maybe you really do need six more months of experience.

- **You may get an offer when you're about to leave.** What if you go to give your notice to quit a job and they make you an offer to stay? Ack! This can be awkward! You were all ready to make your exit, and now they're giving you an incentive not to. You'll have no choice but ask yourself again why you're leaving: Is it for money and advancement possibilities? Then you might want to consider their offer, depending on what they're dangling in front of you. Are you just unhappy with the job? A counteroffer probably won't sway you, unless it's *really* good, and even then you need to be careful about accepting. More money probably won't fix whatever else is wrong with the job for you. Are you leaving to change your career because you have a better job lined up? Then thank them, but decline and proceed with your plans.

- **You may get an offer when you're about to go to another company.** This might be a move of desperation, but if you are planning to move on to another company in a seamless transition, maybe your employer will try a last-ditch attempt to keep you on board. This might seem flattering, but again, you'll have to consider what they're offering versus what you'll be gaining at your new place of employment: the same amount of money or more? A new position and responsibilities? What else will you be getting by taking the new job? Maybe your new company is closer to where you live, or has a better working environment, or is more aligned with your longer-term goals. You'll to consider intangible and nonfinancial factors. But keep in mind, if they're so desperate to keep you now, why didn't they value you as much before?

CHAPTER 2:

NETWORKING ON THE JOB IS THE NAME OF THE GAME

Networking is pretty much what it sounds like: making contact with others to widen your professional and social circle and exchange information that could be of benefit to you and others in the future. Of course, some may define networking entirely differently. One important thing to remember: networking should never be just about what you think you can get from meeting and knowing others. Always go into any new networking exercise with the idea that you are bringing yourself, your talents, and your knowledge to help others. The more you are willing to give, the more you'll likely receive in return (see the first section below for more details). Think of it this way: there is a world of people out there who need your help and your expertise, and proper networking is a chance to offer it. If, by doing so, they offer you something in return, then great! But never make that conditional on making connections and being seen.

Networking is crucial to career success; the more people you know, the more likely it is that your name will get around. But it's important to reach out to the right people and do it correctly. This chapter discusses just how to do that, and make your networking a practice that's fun to do and brings benefits to everyone.

[
"Twenty years from now, you will be more disappointed by the things that you didn't do than by the ones you did do."

—MARK TWAIN
]

NETWORKING IS ABOUT WHAT YOU CAN GIVE, AS MUCH AS WHAT YOU CAN GET

This may come as a surprise, but networking is much more about giving than receiving. Go into it with the idea that you want to serve, to assist, and to improve others, and you'll be approaching it with the right frame of mind. Never just view a new contact or colleague as someone that you can get something from. That attitude is selfish and probably won't do much for you in the near future or the long run. Instead, look to build genuine connections and friendships based on mutual respect and sharing. As your career advances, it's these genuine connections that will serve you, not fly-by-night encounters and attempts to get favors. Here are some important things to keep in mind.

- **Take the initiative when reaching out.** If you want to meet people, make the effort to meet them in whatever way is most comfortable to you. It's easy to get sidetracked by other things, or be held back by fear, self-consciousness, procrastination, and any number of other reasons you concoct to keep from doing it. But if you make the effort to reach out in a genuine and sincere way, you're communicating that you care. This means that you need to spend time researching and learning about your potential new contacts, so that you can have something meaningful to say to them when you *do* reach out. If you doubt this as a strategy, think about how you would feel if someone took the time out to contact you, having read about you and what you do. It would feel great, wouldn't it? So bring some of that good feeling into others' lives, and you'll start building solid relationships right from the start.

- **Make the effort to listen.** Nothing communicates friendship better than genuinely listening to someone and appreciating them. And nothing is a bigger irritant than having to endure someone droning on about themselves in a monologue. Be the first person, not the second. Ask questions and get to know the individual that you're connecting with, and they'll likely do the same for you; you'll learn a lot and enrich your experience. Establishing good mutual communication will be great for both of you, and may lead to collaborations, problem-solving, and any number of other benefits.

- **Be open to receiving and giving advice.** It may be that you've reached out to this person specifically because you have a problem that you need help with. There's nothing wrong with that, but it's also great if you can establish connections based on the help and advice that you can offer to them. Maybe you have the solution to their problem! If you have special skills or knowledge that you can share (assuming this doesn't break any company rules), then you are in a great position to start off a new working relationship.

- **Offer to share who and what you know.** Networking is not just about sharing what you know, but also sharing information about *who* you know. As you build your network, you'll meet some amazing people, and it's very possible that some of them would benefit from knowing each other. If you have a contact in need of a solution that you can't provide, but you know someone who can, put them in touch! Or maybe you know of a conference or event that's outside of your field, but would be of great interest to some of your contacts. Maybe you just discovered a great new app or type of software that could be beneficial to someone in your network. Share the wealth! Always remember to come into your network in the spirit of giving and sharing.

- **Remember to value your contacts.** Your contacts are human beings and deserve your respect, courtesy, and trust. They are never there for you to use to move yourself ahead. If that is your sole focus, you need to rethink that strategy, and soon. Your contacts will likely come from a wide range of backgrounds, each with their own unique story. Value those differences. If you get a reputation for being helpful and reliable, people will talk. But if you get a reputation for just being in it for yourself, people will also talk. And once you've got negative word of mouth working against you, it's going to make future networking that much harder, if not impossible. Guard your own reputation, and make the effort to be professional, courteous, and trustworthy at all times.

> **"Only those who respect the personality of others can be of real use to them."**
>
> **—ALBERT SCHWEITZER**

TWELVE METHODS OF SELF-PROMOTION THAT ARE SINCERE

Everyone wants to promote themselves in some way. Whether we're selling something or just trying to move ahead in our careers, we all recognize the importance of self-promotion. The problem is, with so many people out there trying to do the same thing, it can seem like shouting into a hall where everyone else is shouting. You have to wave your virtual hands constantly to get anyone to notice. Worse, you may be worried that you're coming across as a sleazy salesperson, rather than the nice, awesome person you really are! Self-promotion can feel like a big pain, but there are ways you can be more visible and available without the sales shtick. Here are some ideas.

1. **Offer your help freely.** When meeting new people, tell them what you do and put yourself out there with offers of assistance. New acquaintances will respond much more favorably to "Let me help you if you need it" than they will to "What can you do for me?" Always be willing to give your time and input. You'll soon start to get a reputation as being helpful, and that's worth way more than you telling people about how great you are!

2. **Introduce your contacts to each other.** A great way to build and strengthen your network is to introduce your contacts to each other, especially those who might otherwise never meet. It may be that one of your colleagues

has the perfect solution to a problem that another is having. Put them in touch! You may notice others doing the same for you; wouldn't it be great if someone put you in touch with just the right person at the right time?

3. **Listen and be there.** Nothing will make people lose interest faster than you just droning on about what you do and how it's going to change the world (or whatever your plan is!). Flip it around and ask your contacts what it is that they do; what are their hopes and goals? Where do they see the industry going? What advice would they have? Get them to talk about themselves and be enthusiastic about their stories, and your connection will deepen more quickly.

4. **Let your network know about great people.**

If you are following a blog or podcast that you really like, or if you admire a particular industry leader or innovator who's doing great things right now, let your network know about them. Send an email with a link to their site, their talk, whatever it is that will get them in front of others. If you have a blog, give them a mention. Spread the love; it not only helps out the person whose story you're sharing, it may be of real benefit to others that you know.

5. **Be an expert that people need.** Positioning yourself as the go-to person for particular tasks and problems can be a fantastic way to get your name out there, and let other people know about you. Wouldn't you like to be the one that someone contacts for help on a topic that you know all about? The only thing you have to do is actually be an expert on something! Yes, that's the difficult part, but it shows how the commitment to learning and improving throughout your career can really pay off.

6. **Understand your contacts and their work.** Don't just connect with everyone out there; it may look great to see your number of contacts growing, but it probably won't serve you as well in the long term. Be a bit more strategic. Grow your network by reaching out to people that

genuinely interest you, and with whom you will share a rapport. Seek out like-minded people, get to know them and what they do, and open up to them about your own work. Let the mutual understanding and admiration grow!

7. **Ask for feedback.** It's a great idea to reach out to some of your contacts periodically and ask for their opinions. This could be about almost anything, from a project you're working on to an article you've written. Take what they say on  board and see how it can improve your own work. Soliciting opinions and feedback is a great way to strengthen connections, as well as making you better at what you do. Also, it's likely you'll be asked to do the same at some point.

8. **Be enthusiastic and passionate about what you do.** Your interest and enthusiasm for your work, your industry, and your projects will show in the way you come across in conversations. If you are half-hearted or bored with your own job, why should anyone care about what you have to say? Bring your enthusiasm to every conversation; act like you've just started the job and can't wait to get going!

9. **Seek out collaborations and partnerships.** Having a network is a great way to reach out to others for help and even collaborative work. This is especially true if you are putting together a side business of your own, or have other projects that aren't directly related to your work. Sometimes companies also collaborate on bigger projects. With a good network, the possibilities can be numerous! There will probably be many experts of various kinds in your growing network, so don't hesitate to reach out or ask others if they know anyone relevant to your needs.

10. **Follow up.** If you've reached out or if someone's reached out to you, it's very important to follow up. If you promised to send an email, do it. If you've suggested a phone call, make sure that it happens. If you've reached out to someone you want to connect with, and they haven't responded, give them a few days or up to a week, and then send a follow-up communication. People get busy all the time and forget, or put lower priority items farther down on their list, and it's likely they've just not gotten around to it yet.

11. **Take the time to meet up.** Networking via email, LinkedIn, and even the phone are all good, but what really strengthens a connection is an in-person meeting. Lunch, coffee, an after-work drink—all of these are great ways to meet up and get to know each other. Obviously, this only works locally and maybe regionally. If you're in Halifax and your network partner is in Calgary, it may be a bit of a problem, unless you're both attending a conference in Toronto! Regular in-person meetings may not work, but make the effort to put a real-life face to the name as often as you can.

12. **Be persistent.** Don't give up on networking if you don't immediately make the contacts you would like. These things take time and patience. Let your network grow at its own pace, even if you do want to push it along a bit once in a while. Over time, you'll have a valuable group of contacts that was worth the effort to build.

FIVE WAYS OF NETWORKING ON THE JOB

Much of your networking will be done as a result of your job and your business contacts. On-the-job networking is essential if you want to advance. At first, your network may consist mostly of people at your company, but over time it will be helpful to expand your contacts to people in the wider industry. This is where you have a chance to have new doors opened and to offer your own expertise, but your job is a great place to start. Here are some useful ideas.

1. **Identify those individuals at your company that you want to get to know and reach out to them.**
Using the techniques outlined in this chapter, make the effort to make contact with people who you feel would be helpful, and also whom you could be helpful to. These people may be in different departments, different divisions, or even different branches (if your company has multiple sites). Take the time to learn a bit about them so that when you make contact, you have a valid reason for doing do.

2. **Be reachable.** It may seem silly, but make sure that people know how to get in touch with you, whether that's by phone, your company email, Slack, or whatever method you prefer. When reaching out, make sure that you give people every available option for contacting you; you want to make it as easy as possible! And make sure that you regularly check all of these methods; you don't want to accidentally ignore a potentially important email from a

new contact. Check your spam filters regularly to make sure that nothing you actually want to receive gets caught in them.

3. **Make sure your voice mail is of good quality.** If the person phoning you can't understand what you're saying, you're not going to get very far! Record a short and clear message. Listen back to make sure that it's good enough; if you were phoning you, would your message impress you and make you want to continue the conversation? Have a friend or two phone you and check it out too. You may think it sounds fine, but others may have a different opinion.

4. **Be ready to meet up.** Lunch, coffee, whatever works. If you're in the same building, it should be relatively easy to set up an appointment, and it may happen faster than you anticipated. Always be ready to accommodate someone you'd like to get to know.

5. **Understand that there are different kinds of business networks.** When you move beyond just your job, you will encounter different kinds of professional and business networks. Here are some of the most common:

   - **Casual networks:** These networks are, as the name implies, less structured, and if they sponsor get-togethers, they will usually be more informal, maybe offering a theme for the evening, but that's about it. Chambers of commerce might host these kinds of events, or other local associations might have career nights and meetups for people in a given industry. There may be no purpose for the event other than to mingle, so it might be worth checking these out if you find something relevant to you, since there will be less pressure to make contacts.

   - **Contact networks:** These kinds of networks tend to have more focus and include one each of many different specialists. These are not events open to the public, but rather are groups of people who grow up through recommendation. An example would be a network that has one of everything related to property and houses: a real estate agent, a contractor, a gardener, a real estate lawyer, etc. Or perhaps a network devoted to websites: a writer, a graphic designer, a coder, and so on. It could be an outside network, or even one within a company, made up of specialist employees. The idea is to have a go-to for everything so that the group as a whole can recommend their specialist when any inquiries come their way. You can see the advantages of being a member of one of these networks; it gives you instant credibility and social proof. Obviously joining one of these clubs can take some doing, but if you can get in, it could really benefit you.

- **Social media:** These are obvious as networking tools. LinkedIn is the most preferred choice, but it's possible to use other sites for networking if you do it properly. See chapter 4.

- **Professional associations:** These groups are devoted to a single specialty or industry, and you may not always be able to join them, at least not right away. Or some may be quite expensive to be a part of. But if there is an association that would benefit you and that has people you want to get to know, it may be worth your time to pursue membership in one or more.

HOW TO EFFECTIVELY COLD CALL (AND NOT FEEL SICK TO YOUR STOMACH): NINE THOUGHTS

At some point in your career (and probably sooner rather than later), you're going to need to pick up the phone and call people to introduce yourself. Whether you are in sales, marketing, or just trying to add new people to your network, the phone is still arguably the best way of reaching out and getting a quick response. There's only one problem: for many people, the thought is terrifying, and they'd probably rather have the earth open up and swallow them than go through with it! If you feel like this, you are definitely not alone. Cold calling is not far off from public speaking, which is routinely seen as one of the most dreaded activities someone can be forced to do. Unfortunately, the phone is still a key to business and career success, so you'll have to get used to this idea. The good news is that it doesn't have to be that scary, and much good can come from it. If the idea of making random phone calls makes you shake and quiver, here are some thoughts to help you cope and get you past your worries.

1. **Identify whom you'd like to call and why.** Some
   people may be best contacted by phone, while others are
   more suited to different kinds of communication. If you hate
   phoning, it may be tempting to stick to the method you
   prefer, and that's fine for the most part. But it might be that
   the best way to reach a truly valuable contact is to call them
   up, so you need to be prepared. Remember, you're trying
   to accommodate them. So make a list of your most likely phone
   contacts, and write down what it is you like about them and why
   you want to connect.

2. **Try to identify the best time to reach them.**
   People are busy and often leave their phones off, having
   them go directly to voice mail at work. So you may get
   stuck in an endless string of nonanswers. You may not be
   able to get information about an ideal contact time, but keep in mind that
   some hours of the day will be likely be better than others, no matter who
   the person is. Don't try calling them at 4:45 on a Friday afternoon. They
   either won't answer or you'll probably not get a very favorable response.
   The same goes for 9:30 on a Monday morning. Use your best judgment.
   Lunchtimes and mid-afternoons from Tuesday to Thursday might be your
   best bet. **Never** call them on their personal phones (unless you have
   permission to), especially after work hours or on weekends.

3. **Remember that you're not a random caller.** It may seem
   that way, and sure, the person you're calling doesn't know you, but if
   you're making the effort to reach out by phone, it's because you've done
   your research and know that this is someone you'd like to meet. You're not
   just dialing random people without any preparation, and if you are, stop
   doing that! Be prepared and know why you're calling.

4. **Write a script.** The good news is, you don't have to go into a call just winging it. In fact, that's a bad idea. Always write out a short script of what you want to say, and then be sure to practice it beforehand. Ask a friend to be the contact and react to what you say. Have them give you feedback on what works and what doesn't. They can even role-play the person you're wanting to connect with and create problems for you! You don't have to reinvent the wheel each time; just create a basic script and then personalize it to your individual needs for each call. Just be sure to practice it well enough that you don't sound like you're just reading it off when you actually do call!

5. **Expect someone else to answer.** If the person you're trying to contact is reasonably important (and often even if they're not), you may have to go through a gatekeeper, who will ask you what the call is about and who you are. This can be tricky. If you feel like a nobody, you may not feel you have any right to reach out to them. This is why you need to have the reasons for doing so well mapped out. The answer can be something as simple as, "I just read their recent article on XXXX, and I'd like to know more about [some aspect of it], if he/she can spare a couple of minutes." An honest answer will very often get you through. For goodness' sake, **never** lie about who you are or why you're calling!

6. **Expect to get their voice mail.** With everyone so wrapped up in being busy these days, it's possible, even probable, that you'll get sent straight to their voice mail. If you have a terror of speaking to people over the phone, you may find some relief in this, but it's still keeping you one step away from making the connection. If you do get voice mail, go ahead and leave a message. Keep it brief (half a minute or less) and outline why you are calling. Don't just say "I'd love to talk sometime"; tie something to it. Again, have they done something interesting or written an article? Bring that up, and ask if

you can have a few minutes of their time. Leave your phone number, but also offer to phone back. If they reach out to you, great—but make sure that you **do** actually try again. Wait however long seems right you: a day, two days, and then follow up. You may get their voice mail again. But polite persistence will probably lead to the two of you connecting at some point.

7. **Be ready if you do reach them.** So what happens if they answer? You panic and hang up? Of course not! It's really not so bad, and if you've practiced your script, there's a very good chance that you'll do just fine. Remember, you're not trying to get something from them or sell them something; you're starting a conversation. Tell the person who you are, mention that article or that achievement, congratulate them, and ask if they have a minute or two to spare.

8. **If they say yes.** This is great news! You've stepped up and reached out. Ask your questions and engage them in a bit of talk, but be careful not to take up too much of their time. You can always ask for more time after the initial contact. If they're nearby, maybe you can try to set up a short meeting at their convenience.

9. **If they say no.** That doesn't mean they're rejecting you, it just means that they might be right in the middle of something and can't spare the time. Don't take it personally; they don't even know you. Ask if there's a better time to call or if they'd prefer an email. Chances are, they'll be fine with reconnecting later on or in a different way.

COLD VERSUS WARM EMAILS

Like the phone, email isn't going away any time soon, and it can be invaluable for reaching out to new people when you want to grow your network. It's also great if you hate the phone and want to use the written word instead. But you have to do it the right way because emails have a tendency to get ignored or lost in the shuffle. Here are some thoughts about how to email correctly and get results.

- **Cold emails:** Cold emails are like cold calls, and while they might not have the raw terror of a cold call, they can still be a bit nerve-racking as you struggle to say exactly the right thing. You may feel like you're sending your email off into the void, never to be seen again. Unfortunately, this can often be the case. If you're just sending out mass mailings with little concern for the recipients, they're going to vanish or get caught in spam filters, and honestly they deserve to. The warm email is a much better option.

- **Warm emails:** There isn't really anything magical about this kind of email. It's not necessarily more friendly or conversational. It just means that, like a personalized phone call, you take the time to create individual emails tailored to their exact recipients, so that each one is personal and meaningful. Here's how to do it.

- **Write a good subject line.** The subject line is crucial. If you do something generic or bland, there's a good chance it will get ignored.

If you write something too sensational, it will seem like spam and get deleted. Keep it personal and focused on your recipient: "I loved your new article in XXXX," or "Thank you for the work you've been doing on XXXX." The point is to catch their attention by showing that the email is about them.

- **Make it personal.** Always greet them personally, never with something like "Dear sir" or "Dear madam." You've already lost them if you do that. "Dear Mr. Smith" or "Dear Ms. Rodriguez" is just fine. Be careful about using first names until they get back to you. If they answer with something like "Best, Jim," you're probably fine using it going forward, but keep it formal at the beginning. If you don't know the person's gender or preference, you can use "Dear [their full name]." Lead the email with something about them. Follow up on your subject line, and spell out what it is you admire or are congratulating them on.

- **Get into the body of the email.** Tie in the opening with the purpose of your email. If you have a few questions about something, mention that. If you'd like to talk with them a bit more about an aspect of their work, say so.

- **Add a call to action.** Ask if the two of you can talk on the phone as a follow up, or even exchange emails at their convenience. Keep it brief and simple.

- **Thank them and close your email.** That's really all you need to do to send an effective warm email. Just be sure that you include all necessary contact information in your signature or the body of the email. This usually just means email and phone number. It's unlikely they'll reach out to you via social media, but you can also include your LinkedIn contact information, if it seems appropriate.

- **And now you wait.** The thing about emails is that the recipient may respond in minutes, or not for days, or even longer. This can be frustrating and make you impatient, but you have to keep in mind that most busy professionals still receive an astonishing amount of email, and sorry to say, there's nothing about yours that's really going to stand out. If it doesn't get trapped in a spam filter, they may file it away in a "read later" file and subsequently forget about it. This doesn't mean that they have no interest, or hate you, or anything else; it just means that it's not a priority. If, after a certain amount of time, you haven't heard back, it's OK to send a follow-up message. Keep it brief, explain that you are following up on your earlier email of [given date] and would like a chance to speak with them, at their convenience. As long as you are not a nuisance about this, it's OK to check in with them periodically.

- **Accept that you may not hear back from them.** The unfortunate fact is that you may never get an email reply. Again, this doesn't mean that they hate you; it may just be that they don't have the time, or email is not their preferred means of communication. You may have to change your tactic and try reaching out to them by phone. If you do get through, you might even get a response of something like "Oh yes, sorry! I did get your emails, but I just haven't had a chance to get back to you." It happens. Alternately, they may just be too busy, or not interested in making connections right now or ever. Accept that with grace and move on. Not everyone that you want to connect with will be willing to do so.

FIVE WAYS TO CONTACT INFLUENTIAL PEOPLE

When networking, you want to reach out to people that you can help and who can help you. This will include those who are your peers, but it should also include people that have influence, thought leaders in your industry, and anyone else important that you feel would be worth knowing in the long run. Such people can be a bit harder to connect with, even in this day and age of everyone being online all the time. If you have your sights set on reaching out to an influential and well-known person, here are some suggestions to make it more likely that you'll succeed.

1. **Find out who knows someone that knows them.** In these days of "six degrees of separation," it's entirely possible that you know someone who knows someone who knows this person well. This is especially true if you're not trying to contact a mega-famous person. Do some research and see who might already be in your social network that may have a connection or can open a few doors. A personal introduction will be far better than trying to email or call them out of the blue.

2. **Reach out to the person for an interview.** If you are writing a regular blog (and you should be!) or are contributing to your company newsletter, try reaching out to the person or their representative for an interview. This is a great and sincere way to make a connection that allows you to learn more about them, and share their work with a larger audience. Everyone wins!

3. **Meet them at an event.** This is not always possible, but if the person is giving a talk or holding a meeting, you may have the chance to meet them afterward. In this case, you might want to contact them beforehand, so they know to expect you and can give you a little more of their time. Be aware that a lot of people may have the same idea, and be prepared for the fact that they may not have time for you or can only fit you in for a minute or so.

4. **Be prepared to offer solutions.** You're not just an awestruck fan wanting an autograph (OK, maybe you are, but that's a different circumstance). It's not enough to merely tell them what an honor it is to meet them and expect that you are now "connected." If you can find some problem they are dealing with and offer a potential solution, you'll have a far better chance of getting and holding their attention. Just be sure that you really *can* help them. Making false promises will end up backfiring quickly!

5. **Consider trying out Shapr and other networking apps.** Shapr is a networking app that is designed to put interesting people in touch with each other. The website states that Shapr has an algorithm that "suggests 15 relevant people to meet each day." Some of these might be influential people that you'd like to meet. The app doesn't connect you with anyone who isn't interested in meeting you, only those with a mutual interest. These kinds of apps may be the wave of the future, and have the potential to be a great time-saving way to grow your network.

NETWORKING AT LUNCH OR OTHER CASUAL MEETINGS

In-person networking is a great opportunity to get to know people better. A face-to-face meeting is far more valuable than just exchanging emails or even talking on the phone. You can usually set these up after an initial online meeting or phone call. If you have the opportunity to take your connection to this level, definitely do it! Here are some suggestions to make sure that it goes well.

- **Confirm ahead of time.** A quick phone call or email will do the trick. Even if you haven't heard from them to the contrary, it's a courteous thing to do. Confirm the time and the location, just to be sure.

- **Be on time.** This goes without saying, and is especially true if you are meeting someone important or influential. You don't want to waste their time or present unprofessionally. Make the effort to be there a few minutes early.

- **Dress the part.** Dress nicely. You want to make a good impression. That is all.

- **Be friendly and attentive.** Shake hands, be polite, do all of the usual things you would normally do. Some small talk at the beginning is fine, such as a discussion of what food or coffee to order. Ask the questions you want to ask, and be attentive to what they say. Never interrupt, and answer when asked questions. Get them talking about themselves, their work, and their vision—anything that interests and excites you.

- **Respect their time.** If they only have a half hour, keep to it. Don't run over just because you're enjoying hanging out or want to ask more questions. If things go well, you'll likely have the chance for another meeting.

FOLLOWING UP

After your meeting, even if things went well (or especially if they did), don't just leave it at that. It's essential that you follow up and keep the communication going. Here are some simple steps you can take to ensure that this new connections turns into a valued and long-lasting one.

- **Send an email in the next day or two.** Following up within twenty-four hours is a normal practice and a good one to stick with, while your meeting is still fresh in the other person's mind. This is especially true if you offered to follow up in the meeting or they invited you to do so. Mention something about the meeting that was a particular highlight for you; in fact, make some notes during your meeting of points of interest, so that you can refer back to them in your later email. Make sure that your follow-up email is edited and reads well; you want to continue to make a good impression.

- **Offer some assistance, especially if something came up in the meeting.** If your new contact mentioned some problem that they are struggling with, see if there is some way you can help. Maybe you don't have the solution, but you might know someone who does. Even offering to look around on their behalf will be a good gesture. If nothing else, offer to chat again to trade off ideas and brainstorm. You'll be creating rapport and trust, and will likely earn their gratitude.

- **Try sending a handwritten note.** This small gesture can make a huge impact in today's digital world. How often does this happen anymore? Sadly, only rarely. But it communicates that the person is of real value. Think of how you would feel if you received a personalized note thanking you for your help. Maybe you have at some point. Just make 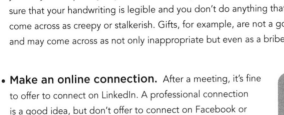 sure that your handwriting is legible and you don't do anything that might come across as creepy or stalkerish. Gifts, for example, are not a good idea, and may come across as not only inappropriate but even as a bribe.

- **Make an online connection.** After a meeting, it's fine to offer to connect on LinkedIn. A professional connection is a good idea, but don't offer to connect on Facebook or Twitter, unless you have a page dedicated to your business or company. Your personal life is not their concern, and theirs shouldn't be yours.

- **Keep in touch.** It's easy, even after a good meeting or two, to get busy and drift apart, but it's important, even essential, that you make some effort to stay in touch with all of your contacts. It probably isn't going to be practical or possible to maintain regular communication with everyone, but even a quick email or message every couple of months is a great way to remind people that you exist, and that you're available to them if they need help, advice, or someone to bounce ideas off. Maybe you saw an article they would be interested in reading or heard about an event they'd like? Have you added someone to your network that you'd like to introduce to others? Simple gestures like this go a long way. Yes, this requires being proactive, and it can be difficult to keep up, but it's worth the effort.

NINE TIPS FOR NETWORKING AT CONFERENCES AND EVENTS

Events are a fantastic chance to meet like-minded people and grow your professional network. These can range from conferences to charity events to product launches, and just about any other kind of gathering you can think of. It's important to see and be seen at these functions, but you need to go in well prepared and have a plan. Just wandering around and hoping to meet cool people won't do you much good. Here are some suggestions for ways to make the most of any kind of event.

1. **Ask yourself what you want to get out of the event.** Obviously, you want to meet people, right? But the bigger goal is to make genuine connections and see what you might be able to bring to the table. You want to present yourself as a helper and solver or problems. It's fine to go into an event with some goals in mind, but keep them limited so that you can focus; "meet everyone" is not a valid or likely goal, but "meet three people in XXXX industry whom I admire and want to get to know better" is quite realistic. You don't have to do everything or be everywhere. Making a few solid connections is far better than making twenty with people you'll never talk to again after the event.

2. **Identify the people you want to meet.** The event will
   probably have people that you're interested in meeting; that's presumably
   why you're attending, right? So do some background research on them.
   Read about them at the company website, check out LinkedIn profiles,
   familiarize yourself with who they are and what they do. This will give you
   a chance to strike up conversations that are meaningful and relevant. As
   mentioned, you might even consider contacting them ahead of time (via
   email, for example) and asking if they'd be willing to meet up at the event.
   That way, you already have an introduction, which takes the pressure off
   making initial contact.

3. **Volunteer to help out.** A great way to get an "in" with
   an event is to offer to help out in some way, whether with
   planning, greeting, hosting, or whatever suits you. It's a great
   way to mingle a bit and get to know new people while acting in
   an official capacity for the event. It may even give you greater
   access to people, such as key speakers.

4. **Be ready for encounters by having your pitch ready.** If
   you don't know what you're going to say, you're going to look unprepared
   and waste others' time. Have a short intro about who you are, ready to
   present to anyone. It doesn't need to be long; in fact, the more concise
   you can make it, the better. As always, focus on what you can offer, not
   on a list of your accomplishments. No one wants to listen to you going on
   about how awesome you are. Show them that rather than telling them!

5. **Be attentive to others.** When you are meeting with people, take
   the time to listen and absorb what they're telling you. Be enthusiastic and
   give them your full attention. Remember how you would like to be treated
   and act accordingly.

6. **Present yourself professionally.** Whatever the nature of the event (anything from a casual affair to a black-tie dinner), be dressed nicely, be well groomed, and be clean. You won't get a chance to make a second first impression, so don't blow it. Look your best and be ready to impress. Overdressing a little probably won't hurt.

7. **Business cards are a must, to have and to receive.** Have business cards professionally printed and ready to hand out. Events are a perfect place to do so, and yes, they're still relevant in the digital age. Having a good business card gives people something tangible and makes you more memorable. It will set you apart if others don't have them. At the same time, be ready to collect business cards from others. When you get a card from someone else, take care of it! Take the time to match the card with the person, even if you need to make a few notes in a small notebook to do so. Be aware that in some cultures (such as Asia) you're expected to examine the card before putting it away. Keep a small case for all the cards you collect and treat them with respect. You'll need to refer to them later when reaching out.

8. **Turn off devices for the duration.** It's important not to get distracted. You're there to get something out of the event, not to check your emails and texts. Turn the phone off and put it away; every distraction will still be there waiting for you after the event. But valuable contacts won't be if you don't give them your full attention.

9. **Follow up as soon as you can.** Don't let potentially great contacts slip away. Make sure that you follow up with them as soon as is reasonable. A short email that lets them know you enjoyed meeting them and would like to stay in touch is enough to keep the conversation going.

NETWORKING ONLINE: NINE WAYS

> The real world is crucial to making solid connections, but there's no doubt that networking online is also very important, even if it's as a prelude to real-life meetings.

1. **Join online professional groups.** Whether on LinkedIn, Reddit, or elsewhere, join up, read through group threads, and be prepared to contribute. But *never* just go in with the idea that you are going to promote yourself! If you show up at a group bragging about yourself or trying to sell something, you'll either be ignored or quickly shown the virtual door. Read, take things in, contribute, and be helpful. Join the community and participate so that people get to know you and welcome you.

2. **Watch what you say.** In professional groups and similar online meeting places, watch your words. Don't act unprofessionally, use profanity, or be overly casual. Also, be sure that your contributions are well-written, edited, grammatically correct, and professional. Others *are* watching what you say, so present yourself at your best at all times.

3. **Find other points of commonality.** Both in groups and in other areas, there will be topics that you have in common with people that make networking easier. Did you go to the same college? Do you belong to any of the same organizations? Do you both volunteer for the same organization or cause? When seeking out new contacts, try to find these kinds of links.

4. **Be clear about why you want to meet this person.** Again, you should not just randomly reach out to everyone. Even after finding commonalities, take a bit of time to think about the reason for reaching out. What value can you bring to this person? What do you hope to gain?

5. **Make effective use of LinkedIn.** It's one of the go-to places for online networking and checking out others. See "More than Just Your Resume: Networking on LinkedIn" on page 103 for more information on how to use the site to best effect.

6. **Make sure you online bio is up-to-date.** It's very important to include all of your latest accomplishments and updates. Whoever is looking for you needs to see you at your latest and greatest. This includes professional photos. Don't put up a picture that is five years old, especially if you'll be meeting people on a regular basis. Keep everything current.

7. **Think about going local.** A great way to start with online networking is to look at groups and online resources that are near you. The reason for this is that once you establish a rapport, it can be much easier to bring things into the real world and plan to meet up. That doesn't mean that you shouldn't reach out to people across the nation and even the world, but thinking small can also bring many advantages.

8. **Offer to contribute to your company's literature.** Does your company have a blog or newsletter? They probably do. Why not offer to contribute something to it? This is a great way to write about something you know that's relevant to the industry, and thus position yourself as an expert. It has the potential to be seen by a lot of people, which increases your visibility and increases the chances that others will start reaching out to you. It also makes it

much easier for you to network with others at your workplace, since they'll already likely know who you are.

9. **Create a website that gives visitors real value.** Having a professional-looking website is a great way to make yourself known, but it can't just be all about you. Think about how you can deliver interesting content and engage your visitors with valuable information to keep them coming back. See "Should You Have a Personal Website or a Blog?" on page 113 for more information.

> **"The real test is not whether you avoid failure, because you won't. It's whether you let it harden or shame you into inaction, or whether you learn from it; whether you choose to persevere."**
>
> **—BARACK OBAMA**

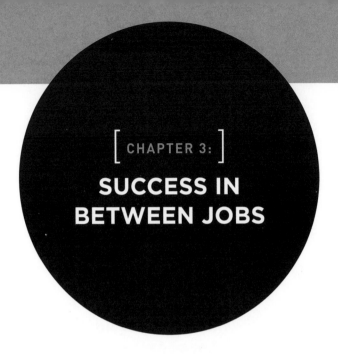

[CHAPTER 3:]

SUCCESS IN BETWEEN JOBS

At some point in your career, you're likely to find yourself between jobs. This may be during an easy period of transition, as you leave one job and enter right into another, or it could be a more stressful time, when you've been laid off or are otherwise unemployed. But not working doesn't mean that you can't be focused on your success; in fact, it's one of the best times to be! This chapter will explore some of the best strategies for making sure that you stay on track for your long-term goals, even when you're not actually at a job.

ELEVEN TIPS FOR HOW TO SEARCH FOR NEW JOBS

Starting a new job search can be overwhelming. While there have never been more opportunities to get out there and look, the bad news is: there have never been more opportunities to get out there and look! The competition can seem fierce (and it often is), the process can be confusing, and you may be stuck with where to even begin. If the whole thing makes you want to give up before you even get going, here are some pointers to get you started, which will be explored in more detail in the rest of the chapter.

1. **Clarify what it is that you want for yourself.** Get very clear in your mind what it is you're looking for. Having a general sense of your ideal job isn't going to do you much good; how will you notice it when you see it? List your requirements: salary, hours, other benefits,  commute, the type of working conditions you want, and so on. You may never get an exact match in the real world, but being clear about your preferences will help you hone in on the most likely jobs for you. Obviously, you can't be ridiculously picky, but being able to weed out those jobs that aren't the best match will save you some time.

2. **Consider all of your options.** As a part of getting clear, range your mind over all of the potential options for a new job. Does it need to be near your home? Can it be farther away (be careful about getting

locked into a long commute, however, or you may regret it later on).
Do you need to work from home a day or two a week? Are you open to
relocating to a new town, city, or even province? Maybe this is the time to
make that change, if you've been considering it. Basically, identify all the
options you are willing to consider.

3. **Make your resume fit each job description.** No two jobs
   are alike, and you'll need to tailor your resume specifically to each. Read
   the job description carefully, look for key words, and work those into
   your resume, if at all possible. Make sure you're not bluffing, of course!
   Have your resume focus on achievements: how you actually helped your
   previous employers, rather than just a list of daily responsibilities. Try to
   make these achievements relevant to the position you're applying for.
   You want to be able to stand out.

4. **Tailor your resume to get past the initial computer
   scans.** As an addition to the above entry, most resumes are read by a
   computer first, which will often eliminate bad matches before a human
   being even looks at them. Then, depending on the size of the company,
   someone in HR may scan it before it gets to the right party. Always make
   sure that you have the right language to match what the job description is
   looking for.

5. **Make use of all of your online options.** There are a
   bewildering number of job sites out there, and a lot of them might be
   a waste of your time. Try to search for your career or industry, and set
   up email alerts for when opportunities matching your criteria become
   available; let the job offers come to you! Watch out for scam sites;
   they're usually pretty easy to spot (often promising large salaries and
   quick results). Also, **never** upload personal information (such as credit
   card numbers). There are many tools on Twitter, LinkedIn, and other sites
   that make the process of getting your resume out there easier. LinkedIn
   groups, for example, can help you connect with people who are employed

at companies you would like to work for. You can reach out to them, provided you do so out of a mutual group interest, not because you're stalking them! LinkedIn, incidentally, is the go-to for most recruiters, so if you're not there, you're really not anywhere! As for getting your resume in top shape, there are sites that will evaluate your resume to see if it will get past the initial computer scan. Use these kinds of tools to take some of the pain out of the search process.

6. **Make use of leads beyond the online world.** There's still a real world out there, so don't get caught up only in the online job searching process. Some of the best jobs available come from word of mouth or because a friend of a friend's company is looking for someone, and you happen to be the perfect fit. These kinds of serendipitous events happen more often than you think, and can give you a real advantage as well as a foot in the door. Again, this is why networking is so important. If you've been cultivating a good professional (and even personal) network, you'll have more opportunities, some of which you would never have heard about otherwise. It doesn't hurt to reach out to companies you'd like to work for directly, even if they're not hiring. Getting your name into their files and showing an interest in their business will reflect well on you, and could help you out at a later point if they contact you.

7. **But also get your online presence up-to-date.** Whether you are focusing online or off-line, it's imperative that you have your resume ready (in several versions) to send out or link to immediately, if someone asks for it. Keep it up-to-date at all times, and add any new and relevant information to it immediately as it happens.

8. **Consider temporary work while you are searching.** If you don't have a full-time job, it may be necessary to do some temp working while you try to remedy that. There are many staffing agencies that need people for jobs that last a few days to a few weeks. It's a

way to make money quickly and keep yourself afloat while waiting for the big prize to come in. Plus, it may even give you a look at some different industries and help you refine your search for a permanent job.

9. **Keep applying.** Don't just apply for one or two jobs and be done with it. Even if you get an interview, you'll want to make sure that you have other proverbial irons in the fire. You may get that job, in which case, great! It's always easier to decline an interview because you've found something else than it is to go into an interview with a desperate mindset, because it's the only thing you have on offer. Applying to different jobs may even let you be a bit more choosy. If you get two offers from two interviews, you're in a much better position. Your only problem then is making up your mind, which is far more appealing that feeling like you're being forced to take something you don't really like, just because it was offered to you.

10. **Devote time to it.** Take the time to really make your job search a main focus, whether you are currently employed or not. If you are unemployed, consider this your new job until the one you want comes along. Don't just spend thirty minutes a day at it and then leave off. Commit to locating the jobs you want and being ready for them.

11. **Be patient.** Job searches can be incredibly tedious and slow. You might luck out and find a perfect match quickly, especially if you have everything ready and have been proactive with your networking and reaching out. But you'll need to accept that it could also take a while, and this can be frustrating and disheartening. Competition is fierce, and there may be a lot of people vying for one position, so presenting yourself at your best and keeping your information up-to-date is even more crucial.

MAKING THE MOST OF ONLINE JOB SITES: SIX TIPS

Online job sites can be a fantastic resource, but they can also be a pain. Yes, you're seeing any number of potential great jobs listed, but so is everyone else. Competition is much heavier when lots of people are viewing and applying for them. But does this mean that you shouldn't use them? No! You should make use of every tool in the toolbox to widen your job search net. Relying only on these sites might be frustrating, but you're not doing that, of course! Here are some suggestions for how to make these sites work best for you.

1. **Try using a job search aggregator.** There are various sites out there that will search and collect listings from other job sites. The whole point is to bring together jobs in your subject area from various locations. These listings can include those from specific company website job postings that might otherwise take you hours to look through and identify on your own. Obviously, this will save you time and potential frustration.

2. **Use topic-specific job boards.** Another way to narrow down your search is to find sites that include, for example, only listings in your industry. This will save you time scrolling through lots of things you aren't interested in. Of course, the narrow focus means that a lot of other people may be using these tools, too. But you can also try searching for jobs by

location, jobs in the private sector versus government jobs, and so on. There are many different ways to customize your searches.

3. **Look for unusual job niches.** You might consider not just looking at a specific industry, but searching for other criteria. There are job boards only for telecommuting, for example, as well as listings for nonprofits and charities. Want to spend a year in the Arctic? Fancy the idea of working overseas? There are places for that, including for specific countries and locations.

4. **Set up mobile job alerts.** Using phone apps for these sites can save you a lot of time. You can make quick searches in between other activities, rather than having to sit down at a computer to begin your search. You can use your phone on public transit, at lunch, or any time to make quick searches and flag anything that interests you; just make sure you're not taking time out of your current job (if you have one) to search for a new one! By setting up alerts, you'll get notifications of anything relevant as soon as it becomes available.

5. **Keep an eye on the posting dates.** While you would think that job boards would want to have only current listings, this is strangely not the case, and more often than you might think. It would be very frustrating to see a listing for which you are perfectly qualified, only to find out it was from eight months ago, but it happens. There are reports that some sites still have job listings up that are a few *years* old!

6. **Look for other information on these sites.** Many job sites have tools, like profiles for companies posting jobs (which allows you to get to know a bit more about them) and what skills are currently trending as hottest and most sought-after (a great way to fluff up your resume with important key words). Some sites list which cities have the largest number of job openings. Search around for this kind of useful extra information.

REACHING OUT TO YOUR NETWORK TO ANNOUNCE THAT YOU'RE JOB-HUNTING

One of the best ways to start job-hunting is to leverage your own networks, both personal and professional. You probably already know far more people than you think you do, and asking some of them for help in your search may yield some surprising results (just make a point to return the favor if you are ever approached). In general, people are happy to help, if you ask. If you're putting yourself out there for a new job, here are some ideas for how to approach those you already know.

- **Create a list of contacts.** If you've already spent some time networking, and you should (see chapter 2), you will have contacts in a variety of areas, from LinkedIn to colleagues at other companies. Go through these and see which ones would be your best bets to reach out to. This may take a while, so don't try to do it all at once. Do a few at a time, and compile a list, maybe divided up into categories: by industry, by job description, or by whatever helps you break a bigger list down into a smaller one. Rank these contacts by order of preference, with the mostly likely contacts taking priority. But don't exclude people just because you don't think they might be able to help. Opportunities often come from unexpected places! These individuals don't have to be close contacts, though it's fair to say that if you connected with them on LinkedIn two years ago but have never said a word to each other since, you're probably not going to have a lot of luck, if you get a response at all.

- **Reach out to people as individuals.** There are differing opinions about this. Some job-search coaches think that it's fine to send a targeted email to a larger group of contacts, provided you make it short and specific. This does have the advantage of casting a wider net sooner and may yield some unexpected replies from people you may not have considered as serious possibilities. On the other hand, if you receive a mass email from someone, even a friend, how much time do you realistically spend looking at it? Maybe you file it away with the intention of responding and then forget about it. But if a friend reaches out to you personally, you're more likely to pay attention. Sending individual emails doesn't mean you have to write a new one every time. Write up a basic template email, and personalize it to the recipient before sending it.

- **Be clear about what it is you're looking for.** Writing to them and saying things like "if you ever happen to hear of anything related to the general area . . ." isn't going to get you much in the way of decent replies. But if you know what kind of position you're looking for, be specific and narrow it down. The more you can be focused, the more likely someone will be able to help you. Yes, this eliminates some possibilities, but it will prevent friends who mean well from sending you leads that aren't a good fit or that you have no interest in.

- **Be careful about whom you contact.** If you are still employed, it's not a great idea to reach out to coworkers. Word travels fast, and unless your boss/company knows that you're leaving, it could get very awkward. On the other hand, if they do know you're leaving (such as moving to another city or province), then don't hesitate to reach out to your current boss and others to see if they have contacts in your new home. They'll probably be happy to help out and may even write you a great reference letter (see page 78).

- **Don't forget your personal friends and family.** This is, strangely, an often overlooked area for job networking. You know your family better than anyone, and they know you, too. If you're in the market for a new job, be sure to let them know. Is your sister working for a really cool company? Tell her you're searching. Does you dad have contacts in his office that might open some doors? Talk to him about it. The same goes for your personal friends; who among them are doing really great things? Who has a job you wish you had? Who might be able to point you in the right direction in your search? You'd be happy to do the same for them, so don't hesitate to ask.

- **Have your resume ready.** Some search coaches recommend attaching it to your message, but this can cause issues with it being flagged as spam if the contact is not someone with whom you are in touch with regularly. Having it online, such as at LinkedIn, can be a good alternative. You can provide the link in the body of the email. Whatever you choose, keep it up-to-date and have it ready for anyone who wants to see it.

- **Remember to follow up.** Give each contact a reasonable amount of time to respond. This may be a few days, but don't just send one email and let it go at that. People get busy and sometimes need reminders. If you've waited three or four days, or a week, and not heard back, it's perfectly acceptable to send a short follow-up email asking if they received your previous message. Some emails get caught in spam filters, and some people skim them with the intent of coming back to them later but then forget about it. On the other hand, don't pester people. A lack of response after twenty-four hours is not an invitation to start emailing them every day. Respect their time. And if someone *does* get back to you with the offer to help, be sure to thank them and offer to return the favor, should they ever need it.

HOW TO APPLY FOR JOBS PROPERLY

The job application process can seem long, drawn out, and a big pain. Unfortunately, it's a hoop you'll just have to jump through in almost every case (unless you're lucky enough to have a friend hire you on the spot!). The good news is, in most cases, there is a fairly standardized and straightforward way to go about applying. As you may know, a job will need certain documents to assess your suitability, a computer may decide your fate before a human being even sees them, and you may have to do a phone interview before you ever get your foot in the door. Assuming that you're going about applying for the job the standard way, here are the reminders of what you'll need.

- **Your resume:** Obviously, this is the most important part of any job application. Your resume is your one-page biography, and tells your potential employer all the key facts about you. You'll want to keep a standard, up-to-date version that you can tweak slightly for each job you apply for. For more information, see "The Perfect Resume" later in this section.

- **Your cover letter:** A cover letter gives you a chance to say a bit more about yourself, to go into a bit more detail than a resume. Each cover letter you write must be specific to the job you're applying for, whereas your resume might just need a little adjustment here and there to tailor it to a specific job. Not every job requires that you submit one, but taking the time to do so will show that you have a genuine interest in the position. It's worth bothering to write, since it will likely make you stand out.

- **References:** Most job applications require references. Usually, you'll need to provide three. These can be from former employers, college professors, work colleagues, or anyone that you feel will be able to give a good evaluation of your skills. For more information on how to acquire quality references, see "Eight Tips when Soliciting References" in the next section.

- **Applying in person:** It's still possible in many cases to drop off your application and related documents in person. If the company or the recruiter is local to you, you may be able to swing by and leave a physical copy of all materials with the appropriate party. However, many companies prefer (or even require) that you submit online. Even if you do submit your application in person, they may also ask you to email them a copy.

- **Applying online:** You may have to email your application to a specific address. If this is the case, try to make your email stand out a bit more by personalizing it. Address the actual recipient, if you know who it is; *never* write "To whom it may concern" or some other ridiculous and impersonal greeting! Alternately, you may have to submit your materials via an online form; many recruiters now require this. One of the more irritating things in the modern job hunt is that you often have to go through and fill out an online form that basically gives all the same information as the resume you will need to attach at the end of it! This is a frequent complaint of many job seekers. It seems stupidly repetitive, and it is. It's usually required because a computer scans your application first, looking for key words in the online form. If it doesn't have enough of a match, your application may be rejected before it ever gets seen by a human being. Therefore, it's important to make sure that you include some of the key words of the job description in your online form: this may include skills, software knowledge, education and certifications, etc. The more that you can do to get past the electronic gatekeeper, the better!

EIGHT TIPS WHEN SOLICITING REFERENCES

References are usually an essential aspect of the job application process. They give potential employers who don't know you a chance to get some more impartial feedback; obviously, *you* think you're great, but they'll need to do more than just take your word for it! A good reference, say, from your manager can be invaluable in securing your next job. So, how do you go about asking for these priceless pieces of paper? What can you do if you didn't leave your last job on good terms with your boss? Here are some tips to get others saying great things about you!

1. **Make sure you deserve it.** It's sound silly, but before you go asking people in various positions, ask yourself if you've done enough to be worthy of their time and praise. If you've not taken your job seriously, gotten in trouble, or had other run-ins with your employer, they may be very unwilling to give you a helping hand on the next phase of your career. This is also true even if it's not your fault. If you've had the boss from hell who made your life miserable, it's not going to do you any good to ask that person for a letter of recommendation.

2. **Find an alternative to your boss, if you need to.** If, as mentioned above, you have a boss who basically has no intention of giving you a good recommendation, you'll need to get a bit more creative. If you have former coworkers whom you got along with, it's fine to reach out to them and ask, provided they're willing to keep it

confidential and not tell your former boss (and if they're friends of yours, they'll probably be fine with doing this).

3. **Search elsewhere for references.** Your recommendation letters don't have to be from your former boss or even your company. What you want is good material that puts you in a good light and highlights your best qualities. Try thinking outside the box: former college professors, satisfied clients, colleagues at other companies who know you and your work, people from places where you volunteer, etc. There is probably a whole list of suitable candidates that you're not thinking of until you take the time to brainstorm and write down some possibilities. Try to come up with at least five to seven potential referees, because almost always a few of them won't work out. You may need different references for different jobs, depending on how different they are; if you want to reuse a letter for another potential employer, be sure to discuss it with the writer. Most will probably be happy for you to modify it as needed, as long as you don't otherwise change the content. Steer away from family members, though, unless one of them has a specific connection to your industry. Offering a prospective employer a nice note from your mother probably won't impress anyone, sorry to say.

4. **Ask in the right way.** Don't just ask for a reference; approach the person by asking if they feel confident that they could write a good letter for you. That way, if they're uncomfortable or unsure, they can politely decline. Also, you'll be narrowing the subject down to a letter that really focuses on your good qualities, from the specific point of view of that person. Someone who can give a bit of detail about your work in the past, your character, and so on, is going to write a much more effective letter than one that just praises you in general.

5. **Give them the right information.** Let your letter writer know what position you're applying for, what it requires, and why you're a good

fit for the job. Send them a copy of your resume, so they can get a better sense of what you're doing, if it's someone whom you're reconnecting with after some time apart. If they know you well enough, they'll be able to tailor the letter to show you at your best. If they're writing a more general letter, at least this will give them some scope for what you're applying for. **Important:** be very sure to let them know the date when the reference is due, and keep after them (nicely!) to ensure that it's written on time. They may be able to give it to you in a sealed envelope (often with their signature across the seal), or they may be required to email it directly to your prospective employer. Make sure you know which format is required, and give your referee the information they need. If the employer has any other specific requests (for instance, about the format of the letter or its length), be sure to let the person know.

6. **You may have to write it.** In these busy days, not everyone has the time to write a letter. You may get a response like "You just write something and send it to me, and I'll let you know if it's OK." This actually happens quite a lot, so you may be doing your own references with a bit of outside help! Is this cheating? Not really, as long as the referee gets to read it and sign off on it; they might even make some suggestions and edits. If it comes from them in spirit and they're fine with signing their name to it, you're not doing anything unethical. But *never* just make up something in someone's name and submit it without asking them! If you know a potential letter writer is busy, you may even consider approaching them with this method. Offer to write it, send them a few key points, and let them pick the ones they want to include.

7. **Be sure to thank anyone who writes for you!** This should be obvious, but never forget basic courtesy. Someone has taken the time to help you out, so you must acknowledge that. A simple email is enough, so let them know that you appreciate their time and effort. You may have to call on them again in the future, and you want relations to be good.

8. **What if the potential employer wants to contact your current boss or supervisor?** This is always a tricky situation, and most employers realize that you may not have yet told your current employer about your possible job change. In most cases, they will ask your permission to do this. If you are making an amicable move and your boss is aware that you are out looking, this is no problem. If the situation is more strained or you'd rather keep it secret, it's fine to tell them so. Most people are reasonable and won't do anything to cause problems. If they absolutely insist in any case, that's a pretty big red flag and may be a good indication that this isn't a company you want to work for.

> **"Every time you have to make a choice about anything, think, 'Does this go toward or away from what I want?' Always choose what goes toward what you want."**
>
> **—BARBARA SHER**

THE PERFECT RESUME

Is there such a thing? Yes, kind of. Your resume and/or CV will look different depending on your industry, and even the type of job you want within your field. You may need to have several different versions on hand, if you're applying to jobs in different industries. It's important to keep them updated with any new achievements, work accomplishments, education, etc. You'll want to have it stored online (LinkedIn and elsewhere) and have it readily accessible to anyone who wants it. Keep it in Word (or similar) and PDF versions as well, to print out easily if you need to. Keep the font size to no smaller than 11 point (12 is preferable), and with margins of no less than about 1.7 centimeters. You can use any professional-looking design you like (there are countless templates online that you can download). As for the actual content, here are the things you absolutely, positively, maybe, probably need to have on any good resume.

- **Your name and contact information.** Put your name, address, phone number, and email here. If you have a relevant website, list it here, but not a personal site. A LinkedIn address is also acceptable.

- **Your primary job skills.** List whatever it is you do best here. This can be any combination that seems right to you, but the point is to highlight your strengths. It's a good idea to list both defined skills, such as any software or programs you have proficiency with (anything from Microsoft Office to SEO to website analytics to hard-coding), and in a separate column, put more general business skills (project management, leading teams and projects, cold calling) that may be useful in the job you're seeking. If you are going for a specific job, try to list skills that match key words in the job advertisement. This makes your resume more favorable to the applicant tracking system (ATS), and it will help your resume to stand out if a computer is scanning it first (which, unfortunately, it probably will be).

- **Previous work experience.** List the businesses you worked for, your job title, the time period of your work (starting and ending dates), and your primary responsibilities. More importantly, list your accomplishments. Did you help the company meet its year-end growth goals? Write that down! Did your efforts help lead to a 20 percent increase in sales? Let the world know! It's not enough to just describe what you did; you need to show how you were great at it and imply that you could be great in this new job, too! The more hard data points you can include here, the better.

- **If you have no other relevant work experience.** If this is your first job hunt and you have no relevant company work experience, put down the other work you've done that might be even a little bit related. This is especially true if you've done volunteer work where you've used some of the same skills, or personal work. Even if you've only worked in coffee shops, you've probably developed some good people skills; that's always in demand. Have you helped your friends and family set up their websites? That could be important. Don't discount "life experience" work, and look for anything you've done that could be relevant to the job. Even having great phone and communication skills is a huge plus.

- **Education.** Depending on the kind of job you're after, your education may be very relevant, or not so much. But list it anyway. Your commitment to getting a degree shows a level of stick-to-it-iveness that is important.

List your GPA, if it is favorable (some companies want to know, though it's usually optional). If you have any professional training or other certificates, list them as well. The more you have, the better you will look.

- **Any additional information.** This is a place to let a little of your personality shine through. Do you speak another language (especially beyond English and French)? Do you have an unusual hobby or interest? Are you an awesome saxophone player? Did you once appear on a television game show? Are you a member of any clubs or professional organizations? Anything unusual will make you stand out and differentiate you from the others who are applying. The point is that you are an individual, not a set of numbers and facts. So let them see a little bit of the real you.

- **Keep it concise.** Unfortunately, all of this needs to fit onto one page, or at most two. You may have to play around with it a little bit to get in everything that you need to, but resist the temptation to make the font or the margins smaller. That will be obvious and might even be disqualifying in some cases. Part of the trick is to get it down to a concise, easy read. You'll find that as you gain more relevant work experience, you can let go of some of the older information that doesn't serve any purpose any more (that job at Tim Hortons can be replaced by the coding work you did for your last company, for example). Read it, reread it, edit it, and make it as perfect as you can. It's going to be the first (and possibly last) thing a potential employer sees, so you need it to stand out and be impressive!

GETTING READY FOR THE INTERVIEW: SIX WAYS TO PREPARE

You've gotten past the computer scan, you've had a phone call from the company, maybe even a preliminary HR interview, and now they want you to come in and talk to an actual human being or two. Gulp! This is both exciting and terrifying. You may have a good shot at the job, but you know that if you screw this up, you'll blow your chance. No pressure, though! There are many different kinds of interviews and many ways to prepare for them, but assuming that you are having a fairly standard interview at a typical company, what can you do to give yourself the best shot? Here are some tips that should work to get yourself prepared, in most cases.

1. **Learn more about the company beforehand.**
   Take some time to visit their website and their social media pages. Learn as much as you can about their products or their mission. Get a feel for the company vibe and culture, if you can. It's good to take in a bit of the hard data if you want to, but it's just as important to get a sense of how the whole place works. That way, you'll be better able to show how you can fit in from the start. You want to build rapport and show that you'd be a great match. If the company has done something impressive recently (launched a new product, secured extra funding, or sponsored an event), be sure to mention it in the interview.

2. See if you can find out who will conduct your interview. It might be the person who will be your boss, or in a larger company, it might be someone from HR. There may be more than one interviewer. Sometimes, the boss and a few senior employees might be present to check you out. You'll be better able to anticipate how to answer if you know who's going to be asking the questions.

3. Be sure to practice your answers beforehand. Run some trial interviews; maybe get a friend to participate and role-play the whole thing. Write down your answers and have them on hand; it's OK to use notes to practice. Commit things that seem important to memory, so that when the real interview happens, you'll feel more ready.

4. Know your own resume. Make sure that you know all of the information on your resume and any supporting materials. You'll likely get asked about various things on it, and you want to be able to answer with confidence and clarity.

5. Have an extra copy of your resume and other materials. They should have your resume already, but in the real world things go missing, especially if you're one of several interviewees they'll be seeing. You don't want to waste time having them fumbling around for documents, or having to leave and go find it. Give them your extra copy and you'll not only be good to go, but also you'll look prepared and impressive!

6. Decide what you will wear. Don't just pick something on the day of the interview; decide on your clothing well in advance. Always dress professionally and in line with the company's dress code. Check their website to see if there are photographs and other indications of the kind of clothing expected. A tech firm may be business casual, while a law firm will be quite formal. In any case, consider going with a more formal look. It never hurts to overdress for an interview!

TWELVE TIPS FOR ACING YOUR INTERVIEW

You're there! You're sitting in the interview. One, two, or more people are sitting across the table from you, and are ready for you to tell them why you're the best fit for the job. And there's no place you'd rather be less! Well, this may be true; your heart might be racing, you may be sweating, you might feel like you're going to pass out, and your stomach may be in knots, but those are all good things! They are normal reactions to stressful situations. A job interview is a kind of performance, and if you're terrified of public speaking, then you're going to have a rough time of it. But there are many things you can do during the interview to present yourself in a good light and show them just how amazing you are! Here's a useful list to get you started.

1. **Be on time.** There is possibly nothing more important than this. If you are late without good reason, you've probably blown your chance. So do whatever you have to do to make sure that you arrive a bit early: check transit times and traffic. If you are delayed due to traffic or for some other legitimate cause, be sure to phone the company, apologize, and let them know about when you expect to arrive.

2. **Follow basic manners.** Be clean, well-dressed, shake hands, and address everyone politely. During the interview, sit up straight and give

the interviewer(s) your undivided attention. Basically, practice all those good manners you were told to use as a child.

3. **Take a few deep breaths beforehand.** You might be nervous, your heart might be racing, but if you can, try to bring yourself back to the moment, rather than worrying about how it will go; you'll feel better. Deep breathing is an effective way to give yourself a feeling of calm. Find some online resources for breathing or even meditation, and maybe try practicing for a few days before the interview.

4. **Leave your cell phone off.** Always. Unless you are expecting an urgent family update or something similar, the phone stays off and put away.

5. **Be enthusiastic right from the start.** How you present yourself in the first few minutes of the interview will likely set the tone for the rest of it. If you seem disinterested or come off as rude, you've damaged your standing in their eyes before it's even started. Present yourself as happy to be there and grateful for the interview. Never be negative or say anything bad about your previous employer, even if you hated the job! You don't want to seem difficult; you want to make this process as easy as possible for the interviewer.

6. **Give your attention to each interviewer.** If you are being interviewed by two or more people, be sure to give each of them equal time. Make eye contact and answer their questions with equal detail and enthusiasm. Never just focus on the lead interviewer; the others are there for a reason.

7. **Be prepared for behavior questions and action questions.** You may be put on the spot and asked how you would respond in certain situations, or how you did react if it happened to you in the past. This is to test how you would do on the job, and means it's

probably a situation that comes up for them from time to time! It's tough to anticipate these beforehand, but try to think of some ways that you solved problems in the past that might be relevant to this job. If they don't ask, you can volunteer. Stories from the trenches are especially good.

8. **Accent your best attributes.** You're not the only one being interviewed, so make sure you have a small list of the things you feel make you stand apart. What makes you great at what you do, and why should they choose you over someone else?

9. **Ask questions.** It's fine and even expected that you will have questions along the way. Have a set of them prepared beforehand, but it's also fine to jot others down as the interview proceeds; there may be any number of things you didn't think of. You want to know as much as possible, because you're seeing if this job is a good fit for you, too, so don't feel that you can't ask. Asking questions shows that you have a genuine interest in the company and what the job requires.

10. **End on a good note.** Make sure the interview ends with a positive and cordial feeling. Smile, shake hands, and thank the interviewer for their time and for giving you a chance to be interviewed. After the interview, it's always important to send a quick follow-up email thanking them again for their time.

11. **Be mindful of unlawful questions.** It probably won't happen, but there are a number of questions that the interviewer is not allowed to ask you. These include questions about race, ethnic and national origin, First Nations status, sex and gender, sexual orientation, marital status, if you have children (or plan to), religious beliefs, political opinions, disabilities, and so on. If for any reason, one of these topics comes up, you are not obligated to answer it and instead should say something like

"I don't think that's relevant to this interview." You may feel angry or hurt, but it's best to remain polite and try to let the interview proceed; it may not have been intended to upset you or be used as an illegal selection technique. A simple answer such as this should be enough to send the message that they are treading into unlawful space. If they persist or ask other questions, you should probably reconsider working for them; would you really want to work for a place that's already making you feel uncomfortable? It may be worth reporting them to the appropriate authority in your province.

12. **Be prepared for a second interview.** It may be that there is more than one round of interviews. If you get a call to come back in, that's great news! It means that you passed the first hurdle and are now a more serious contender. It's a great chance to correct any minor mistakes you may feel you made during the first interview. They will probably ask you more detailed questions or maybe give you additional scenarios to work through, so be ready and be encouraged!

> **"Success is the sum of small efforts, repeated day in and day out."**
>
> **—ROBERT COLLIER**

YOU GOT THE JOB! WELL DONE! NOW WHAT?

You passed the interview with flying colors, they said they'd be in touch, and now they are, and they're happy to tell you that you've got the job! Excellent! So, what happens next? Well, before the big money starts rolling in, there will be any number of mundane things you'll have to deal with: assessing if this is the job you really want, paperwork, orientation, and other onboarding procedures. Each company will have its own specifics (and some will likely make a bigger deal out of it than others), but here is a list of the probable subjects you'll need to navigate through on the way to perfect job land.

- **Ask yourself if this is the job for you.** Yes, this may seem strange, but if you've done more than one interview, this job may not be your first choice. It's always worth going through the interview process, but now you'll have to ask yourself the big question: Do you actually want this job? Maybe you're waiting to hear back from another possible employer; how much time do you have to make your decision? If you can weigh this job against another, try to do so before committing.

- **Explore (again) the pros and cons.** No job is perfect (well, maybe there are a few, but they're rare!). You'll need to again look at what you like and what you like less about the job on offer. Does it pay enough? Is it close by, or will you have a long commute? Are you comfortable with the culture, dress code, and so on? If you only get one job offer, you may feel like you have to accept, no matter what, but this isn't always the best idea. Be clear as to what is going to be great and what is going to be not-so-great if you take the job.

- **Find out what's negotiable and what isn't.** The job may be great, but it may not pay as well as you'd like. Or the pay may be great, but it's going to take you ninety minutes each way to commute. Is there room for a bit of salary negotiation? Can you work from home a day or two per week? It may well be that you have to accept the offer as-is, in which case, you'll need to sit with it and go back to step two. Depending on your experience, you may be able to ask for more, but be careful about seeming too pushy, or they may just withdraw the offer if you come across as not a team player.

- **Be ready to make a final decision.** Unfortunately, you probably won't have the luxury of thinking about it for too long. If you go ahead and sign a work contract of some kind, and then two days later a better offer comes along, you're kind of stuck. It might even be illegal for you to back out and certainly won't make you look good in any case. At some point, you'll just have to make a choice and be good with it.

- **Prepare for paperwork.** Invariably, there will be forms to fill out. At the very least, you'll need your Social Insurance Number (SIN) to work legally. If you're not a Canadian citizen, you'll need to prove that you can work legally in the country. You'll need one of the following, which allows you to apply for your SIN:
  - A Permanent Resident Card
  - A Confirmation of Permanent Residence
  - A Record of Landing
  - A Verification of Landing
  - A Verification of Status

Once you have your SIN, your employer will take care of the necessary paperwork; they are required to record your number within three days of you taking the job. If you have any questions or concerns, talk to your employer as soon as possible.

ADDITIONAL PAPERWORK

- **Tax forms:** You will need to fill out the TD1 form (Personal Tax Credit Return), both the federal form and one for your province and/or where you'll be working. These forms determine how much tax will be deducted from your pay. If you are employed in Quebec, you'll need to fill out the TD1 for the federal and Form TP1015.3-V (Source Deductions Return) for the province. If you have any questions, ask your employer or refer to the government tax site (see Resources).

- **A job contract:** Not every company uses these, but they are fairly standard in a lot of industries. This kind of contract lays out the terms of employment, your duties, hours, and compensation, any additional benefits, and so on. It may also assure the signer that the job complies with all federal and provincial labor laws. These forms serve as legal protection for the company, so that there are no later misunderstandings, and no disgruntled employees can take legal action against them, claiming that they were deceived about the job description. If you have one of these, be sure to read it carefully and make sure you understand all of its points.

- **Proprietary agreements.** Depending on the kind of company you are working for, you may be required to sign a binding agreement that you will not discuss or share certain things about your work. This is effectively a nondisclosure agreement, and may be legally enforceable up to and including fines and imprisonment. Very often the agreement continues beyond your term of employment and may extend indefinitely. Companies that engage in scientific research (and acquire patents), are defense-oriented, or even just have an important brand they want to protect from competitors are all examples of places where these kinds of agreements are common. You will be expected to take the document seriously and likely say nothing about your job outside of work.

ADDITIONAL PREPARATIONS

- **Orientation and onboarding:** Before you start the job, or maybe from the first day, you may have to attend some form of orientation. This will vary widely from company to company, and it may last a day or even a week, depending on the learning curve and your responsibilities. You may not be the only new hire, and it is a chance to get you eased into the company, meet some of the key people, and get a feel for the company. Make sure that you show up on time and are prepared. If you have any questions about preparation, be sure to ask ahead of time, whether that's through your new boss, HR, or whoever is the appropriate contact.

- **Arrive early:** Not too early, but you want to give yourself enough time to not have to rush and feel stressed. Sometimes, orientations start a bit earlier (say, 8:30 a.m. instead of 9:00), so you'll need to be there earlier anyway. Make sure that you've mapped out your commute beforehand and practiced it. Be sure that you get a good night's sleep the night before, so that you can be at your best from day one. Showing up zonked, tired, and sluggish isn't going to be a good look!

- **Dress appropriately:** Make sure that you know the company dress code and dress accordingly. One of the worst faux pas you can make is to show up underdressed! However, being a little overdressed on your first day (if the company is more casual) won't do any harm. You can always see what everyone else is wearing and dress down accordingly from then on.

- **Make a commitment to meeting people and learning names.** This can seem overwhelming at times, especially if you're not good at introductions and remembering names. But making the effort will do you good in the long run. This topic is beyond the scope of this book, but for more information, see *This Book Will Teach You to Start a New Job Strong*, also in this series.

"Would you like me to give you a formula for success? It's quite simple, really: Double your rate of failure. You are thinking of failure as the enemy of success. But it isn't at all. You can be discouraged by failure or you can learn from it, so go ahead and make mistakes. Make all you can. Because, remember, that's where you will find success."

—*THOMAS WATSON*

You passed the interview with flying colors, they said they'd be in touch, and now they are, and they're sorry to tell you that you didn't get the job. Darn it. Now what? Sadly, you can't always get what you want. You may have had your heart set on one job and got so close you could taste it, only to have it snatched away. Rejection is all too common, but unfortunately, it's just something you're going to have to learn to live with. It never really gets any easier, but you can learn not to take it personally, because it rarely ever is (that's the one bit of good news). This section looks at this unpleasant outcome, why it happens, and what you can learn from it. It may not take away the sting of not getting a job you wanted, but at least you'll understand and be prepared the next time.

- **Thank them for considering you.** Regardless of the outcome, it's always good for you to write a quick email thanking them for the opportunity. It's simply good business courtesy and will reflect well on you.

- **Keep in contact (if you really like the company).** Consider also that they may have need of someone with your talents in the future, and if you're courteous and keep the lines of communication open, you may be at the top of the list the next time they are hiring. It's fine to ask to be considered for other positions in the future, if you'd like to be on that list.

- **Ask for feedback.** A lot of companies won't let you know why they hired someone else. This is often for their own legal protection. They don't want to say anything that could be construed as discriminatory and used against them later on by a disgruntled individual who didn't get the job. But they might give you some pointers that you can use. Take everything they do tell you on board, being mindful that it's still just their opinion. They obviously thought that someone else was a better fit, and that may be the only information you'll ever get from them. Sometimes, it really just does come down to a small difference between you and another candidate.

- **Be upset.** Really, it's OK. There's nothing wrong with being disappointed, frustrated, or angry. If it's a job you really wanted, it's going to be a blow, and it's important to go through that process. Treat yourself to a chocolate something-or-other, have a good glass of wine or two, commiserate with friends and family, and do what you need to do to get past it. But don't let it get you so down that you stop looking for other opportunities. As the saying goes (more or less), each failure is another stepping-stone on the road to success.

- **Remind yourself of your successes.** When you're feeling down about being rejected, it's important to remember the things that have gone well for you and the successes you've had. If you're feeling defeated, start writing down all your accomplishments, and remember the good things that have happened to you. This can be a very good way to put things into perspective. Yes, you didn't get the job, but you are capable of many great things, and other jobs will come along!

- **Remind yourself of what it was about this job that appealed to you.** Keeping in mind what made this job seem great is important, because it will keep you focused on looking for future opportunities that have similar qualities. You may be tempted to just take the first offer that comes along, if you've had a string of failures, but this is not usually the best idea. Always remember what your goals are, and try to look for new listings that match them. You'll be much happier in the long run if you can find the right match.

- **Don't dwell on it.** You may be tempted to stew over it and think about every word you said, what you might have done better, or what you might have said that could have swayed them, but this is a waste of your time. The more you dwell on what might have been, the less you'll be able to move on. The truth is, you may never know exactly why they chose someone else, even if they gave you feedback, so don't get caught up stressing over it. Yes, maybe you could have said or done something different, but you'll never be sure, so let it go. One rejection doesn't make you a failure. Five rejections don't make you a failure. It's all just part of the process.

- **Let failures and setbacks be useful and instructional.** If the interview didn't go your way, use the experience as a learning tool. What can you take away from it and what can you learn? How can you use that to your advantage for your next interview? Each setback can be very valuable in giving you insights into how you can improve. Think about what you feel you did right versus what you could have done better. In what ways can you improve so that your next application and interview goes better? Always be looking for how you can improve.

CHAPTER 4

ACHIEVING SUCCESS ONLINE

The online world drives everything these days, it seems, and you simply won't get far if you're not making use of it to the fullest extent possible. The internet can be a phenomenal waste of time if you don't use it properly, but a great asset if you make a real effort to get out there and network. From the pitfalls of social media to the benefits of having your own website, this chapter will talk about various actions you can take to connect with others and make your time online really count.

THE POTENTIAL MINEFIELD OF SOCIAL MEDIA: SIX THINGS TO WATCH OUT FOR

Social media has changed forever how we interact with each other, which is both a blessing and a curse. Sites like LinkedIn can be great for making new contacts and growing your network, but some social media platforms can also be ridiculous time wastes and give you nothing of value in terms of advancing your career. There are countless dos and don'ts when it comes to social media etiquette. Your workplace may already have regulations in place. Here are some important things to keep in mind and look out for when using social media on the job.

1. **Watch how you interact on official pages.** Your company may have dedicated pages on various social media sites, so be careful what you post if you are on them. As an employee, you represent your company, and a sure way of making yourself look bad is to post something unprofessional to the page. If you are in charge of content for any of the company's social media pages, you have to be especially careful about what you post at all times, and everything listed below is even more important.

2. **Personal pages must stay personal.** Stay off your personal social media pages at work. A lot of companies already have policies about not doing this, so abide by them. Also, if you have a dedicated

work email address, never use it for personal purposes, much less to create a personal social media profile!

3. **Watch what you post about work on your personal profile pages.** It's probably better if you don't post anything work-related, beyond your position and what you do, but be especially careful about not criticizing your company, or discussing new projects and anything proprietary. Even if you're not planning on staying there in the long term, doing this could get you fired or even make you the subject of legal action.

4. **Don't talk about office politics on your profile.** Even if you have the most annoying coworker in the world, resist the temptation to post about it on your personal page. Likewise, don't spread office gossip online, even if you don't name names. Eventually, someone will see what you're doing.

5. **Don't criticize your company's competition.** This may seem like it's not a big deal; after all, you're standing up for your own company. But it looks unprofessional and could still reflect badly on your workplace, sending the message that they encourage their employees to talk badly about others.

6. **However, be mindful of your rights.** Your employer has the right to insist that you not access your social media profiles on company time. But they do not have the right to request or demand access to your profiles, unless there is suspicion of criminal activity. They cannot ask for your passwords or insist that you log in while your boss is watching. This is true even at the start of your job. If an interviewer wants this information,

allegedly for HR or some other department, it could be an attempt to discriminate against you based on what they find in your profile. You may have the right to file a complaint with the appropriate provincial authority. See the Resources section for more information.

[
"Nothing will work unless you do."

—MAYA ANGELOU
]

MORE THAN JUST YOUR RESUME: SIX POINTS WHEN NETWORKING ON LINKEDIN

LinkedIn offers many great ways to reach out to like-minded professionals and make genuine connections that can benefit everyone. Of all the social media sites out there, it's the one best suited to growing your professional business network. As with everything online, there are things you should do and things you shouldn't. Here are some suggestions for how to get the most out of LinkedIn and use it effectively.

1. **Keep your information current.** Your profile is what people are going to see, and they need to see the best version of you. Consider your page a brochure and a resume rolled into one. Have a current profile picture and always add new information. Try to do a weekly update, if you can. Just remember to turn off notifications when you're updating, so that others don't have to read about it!

2. **Keep your information clear.** In your profile, make sure that you describe what you do at the top of the page. Use clear language, none of that "Empowering today's B2B visionaries by converting each 'no' to a 'yes'" garbage. Seriously, everyone laughs at language like this, so don't use it. You'll look like a pretentious jerk. Be clear and direct.

3. **Be mindful of etiquette in groups.** Join groups that you have a genuine interest in, not those that you think are going to be of use somehow. Be active, but don't just post about yourself. The point is to bring your value to others and contribute; over time, you'll gain a reputation for being helpful. As with any online group, be respectful of others. Never spam and never join a group just to start advertising yourself. You'll probably get kicked out very soon.

4. **Be careful when viewing profiles.** Change your setting to anonymous if you don't want them to know that you're looking at their page. This is especially true if you go back to view a profile more than once. The last thing you want is to be seen as stalking someone, which will ruin your chances of networking and could upset and alarm the other person.

5. **Strive to make genuine connections.** Don't just connect with anyone and everyone. The generic "join my network" approach gives others no real reason to connect with you. Reach out to others in groups first, start a conversation, develop a rapport, and build a relationship. Then when you connect, it will be far more meaningful.

6. **Give real testimonials and endorsements.** Be prepared to take some time to talk up the people you are connected with. A good and honest testimonial is worth a lot to someone, and they'll be more likely to endorse you properly in return. Social proof on LinkedIn, as in life, makes a difference, so take some time to praise those that impress you.

MORE THAN JUST MEMES: FIVE TIPS FOR USING FACEBOOK

Though it has been criticized for its privacy issues and data breach problems, Facebook has some use when used professionally for networking. Your company may have a Facebook page (or more than one). You may decide to create your own professional-based profile or page to reach out to like-minded individuals and organizations. Here are some things to keep in mind when using this gigantic platform.

1. **Always keep your professional and the personal pages separate.** Never use your personal Facebook page or profile for professional purposes. Create a separate page devoted to your work only. Use professional photos, post business-related content, and treat it as an extension of your company, because it is. You might be able to use your company's logo and designs, but always ask first, to avoid any legal problems.

2. **Decide if you want a profile or a page.** Both have advantages and disadvantages, but a page might be the better option. It will look more professional, and you can fill it with relevant work information. Having page "likes" rather than profile "friends" may also present better.

3. **Add the needed information for your page.** Be sure that your About page includes a summary of who you are and what your work

is all about. Make sure to include any relevant contact information. As with LinkedIn, include a page photo that's up-to-date.

4. **Use your page well and often.** Post regular updates that engage readers. Try to get them to share your content, since this boosts the page's reach and will potentially bring you more likes. Facebook has a number of tools to help with engagement; you don't just need to pay to boost your post reach. Study your analytics to see what kinds of responses your posts are receiving. Always answer any messages promptly and professionally. Be active and engaging.

5. **Don't use your page to sell yourself or anything else.** Just posting about how great you are or how great your company is won't impress anyone, and you might start losing the likes you do have. Have a defined sense of what your page is for and stick to it. Post things that are relevant to your followers. Share interesting articles and videos that will be of use to your followers. Post regularly, every day if you can. Connect with other pages and partner with them to post engaging content. The idea is to build a network by offering information that people can use or at least be entertained by.

> **"Successful salesmanship is 90 percent preparation and 10 percent presentation."**
>
> **—BERTRAND R. CANFIELD**

HOW TO TWEET TO WIN: TEN TIPS FOR USING TWITTER

As with Facebook, may companies have a Twitter account, and many businesses are quite active on the site, posting regular updates and links. Your company may already be doing this with its own page. If you want to have a professional Twitter profile devoted to your work and your company, here are some ideas for how to make it work for you.

1. **Make your page as professional as you can.** There isn't too much you can do to customize a Twitter page, but the usual ideas still hold: have a professional photo, write a clear, brief description of what you do, include relevant contact information, and keep it simple.

2. **Follow other businesses and individuals that interest you.** Keep this page for business only, and don't start following entertainment pages or celebrities unless they are related to your business. Also, you're not obligated to follow back everyone who follows you. Follow those with whom you'd like to make a genuine connection.

3. **Post regularly.** You should try to post every day, even a few times a day if you can. Make sure that you limit your posts to topics that are business-related and that your followers will find interesting. The occasional off-topic or humorous post is fine, but don't get too distracted by irrelevant links and content. Avoid personal interests and controversial topics like politics, unless a political event is directly related to your

industry. Don't post about yourself constantly. The occasional brag about an accomplishment is fine, but make sure you give your followers things that will interest and be helpful to them.

4. **Use hashtags.** Twitter is great for hashtags, but be mindful not to overdo it. Even without the 280-character limit, adding several hashtags looks sloppy and unprofessional. Keep it to two or three at most, and make sure they are relevant and will increase the chances of your post being seen.

5. **Be brief.** Your comments don't need to be overly long, and you probably shouldn't let them run on for multiple tweets. Sometimes a longer thread can be useful if the topic is more in-depth, but it probably won't increase your engagement unless you already have a large and/or devoted following.

6. **Don't post long URLs.** These take up a lot of valuable character space. There are various sites online that take a longer URL and condense it to save space, so run the longer ones through one of these before adding them to your tweet.

7. **Ask questions.** Asking your followers questions about themselves, their work, and their interests is a great way to stimulate response and increase engagement. Maybe ask them to introduce themselves to everyone? Maybe try a poll about something?

8. **Make comments on any retweets.** Let your followers know why you are sharing a particular tweet or link. Again, it should be relevant to your interests and theirs, so make sure that you tie it all together.

9. **Pin an important post.** If you have something that you want more of your followers to see, pin it at the top for a few days or a week to increase its visibility. Change these up from time to time, so that anyone coming to your page isn't just seeing the same post over and over.

10. **Edit before posting!** It's essential that your posts be professional-looking, well-written, and edited. Make sure that you read through each post before it goes out, because you can't fix it once it's up. Your only option is to delete and start over, which is irritating, to say the least.

> **"How much easier our work would be if we put forth as much effort trying to improve the quality of it as most of us do trying to find excuses for not properly doing it."**
>
> —*GEORGE W. BALLENGER*

INSTAGRAM FOR SUCCESS? SURE, WHY NOT? (SEVEN TIPS)

Instagram may not seem like the most obvious choice for professional networking, but it can yield some interesting results. As with other forms of social media, it requires regular posting and patience to build a following. Here are some ideas for using it to network.

1. **Make the effort to post regularly.** It can be every day or three times a week, but try to keep it on a schedule. If you only want to post three days a week, always post on the same three days every week. Try to post at the same times, too, or close to them. Be careful about over-posting, though. Twice a day is enough, unless you get really famous!

2. **Make your one link count.** With Instagram, you can only post one outside link on your page, so make sure that it's to something useful, such as your business website, your company's site, or your LinkedIn page. You can change it whenever you like, but it's probably best not to switch it out too often. Advertise the link in your posts when it's relevant (write "link on bio page," or something similar), but don't post that every time, or you'll look like you're selling something.

3. **Use hashtags.** Hashtags are crucial on Instagram, so use them frequently and strategically. Decide on key words that are relevant to your post and add them in to get more potential viewers. Don't go overboard with an absurd number, like fifty, but adding five to seven relevant hashtags

is a great way to amplify your post a bit more. Searching hashtags will also let you discover other accounts that may be of interest to you and worth following.

4. **Post relevant content.** As with other social media professional pages, keep your account on topic and make all posts related to your business themes. Don't post random pictures of your vacation or funny things you find online, and no one cares about what you're eating. If you can't post something new and interesting for your followers every day, then post less often. Quality is always better than quantity.

5. **Follow other accounts you like.** It doesn't guarantee that they'll follow you back, but it does often happen. If you're following someone and want to get their attention . . .

6. **Comment on posts.** Engage with other accounts and comment on their posts. This is especially true if the post doesn't have a lot (or any) comments; you'll increase your chances of being seen and starting a conversation.

7. **Be careful with Instagram pods.** These are groups set up elsewhere (such as Facebook) to help boost each other's posts. It sounds good in principle, but there has been some backlash against them, since the boosted engagement isn't entirely authentic; it's essentially trading likes for likes. There's some reports that Facebook (which owns Instagram) has been cracking down on groups devoted to this practice. It could be a bad look if you're found to using one of these to try to get seen more.

OTHER SOCIAL MEDIA PLATFORMS

The number of social media platforms is increasing all the time and shows no signs of stopping any time soon. Beyond the biggies, there are a number of up-and-coming sites, some of which already have substantial numbers of users. These may or may not be worth your time, depending on your industry and what you are trying to achieve career-wise. Here are a few of the more popular recent ones, but newer sites are appearing regularly, and this list will necessarily be incomplete in the near future.

Snapchat may be worth your time, if your business and career aims cater to the demographic of teenagers to mid-thirties. People in those age groups are the predominant users of Snapchat. Since stories only last for twenty-four hours, you need to keep your message clear and concise. Snapchat offers a chance to be a bit more creative and fun, but for serious business contacts, it may not be your best bet.

Other platforms such as Messenger and WhatsApp can be useful for staying in contact with people in your network. WhatsApp allows for business profiles, and since both are owned by Facebook, they can integrate with the bigger Facebook platform. If you are interested in networking farther afield, particularly in Asia, you may want to explore apps such as QQ, Qzone, and WeChat, all of which are based in China. TikTok is another recent Asian platform, and like Snapchat is largely geared toward younger users. Its potential for business is unsure as of the time of writing, but, like many other new and emerging social media sites, keep your eyes open for the latest thing. Getting in to a new platform early can allow you to leverage new technologies to your advantage.

SHOULD YOU HAVE A PERSONAL WEBSITE OR A BLOG?

If you want to advance your career, having a business website can be very helpful. So the answer to this section's question is most definitely yes! Your website doesn't need to be extensive and have tons of bells and whistles, but it does need to look professional and be easy to navigate. Think of it as an online business card and a brochure that tells the world about you and your work. It can position you as an expert in your field, and you can offer visitors various helpful resources, such as a blog, links, articles, and so on. Here are some ideas for making the most of your website.

- **Choose your domain name.** This first step is obviously one of the most important. In these days of dwindling name options, you still need to have something that is unique, recognizable, and not too long or difficult to remember. And yes, it's frustrating if you pick the perfect name, only to find that it's already taken, so be flexible and have more than one choice, or find a way to make yours a variant of an existing name.

- **What will your website do for you?** What's the point of this website? It's not for personal use, so what do you want it to do for you? What do you want it to offer to others? Make a list of things that you want your site to feature that will make it stand out.

- **Build your site.** Whether you create it yourself from one of the many programs available out there or hire someone to do it, don't skimp on this step. You need something that is inviting and appealing, but that also looks professional and up-to-date. A design and functionality from 2005 isn't going to cut it these days. If you're "retrofitting" an older website and repurposing it, just make sure the design is current. Many older sites don't work at all on cell phones (or at least look terrible!). Yours needs to be clear and easy to navigate. Lay off the auto-start video; many people find these annoying and they bring to mind the bad old days of the internet in the 1990s, when pages would auto-load music and animations. Keep it simple and minimal. You are the subject of the site, not the bells and whistles and fancy tech.

- **Shouting from the rooftop: getting your site noticed.** One of the biggest problems once you have a website is simply getting anyone to visit it. These days, everything is about SEO (Search Engine Optimization). Everyone wants it, everyone offers it, and everyone seems to think it's some magical solution to all of their problems. It's simply a way, as the name implies, of getting your website up near the top of search engine results. Everyone online is scrambling for attention, so you need to be able to make your site stand out. You want to include key words that reflect what you do, but that aren't so generic that there's nothing original or individual about them. Try researching what your colleagues use, and see if you can formulate a list of key words that works for you. Try to make some of them very specific to you, if you can. The point is to position yourself as an expert and someone who might have the solutions that others need.

- **Keep your site updated.** As with your LinkedIn profile, it's essential that you not let your website get out of date. How many times have you gone to a so-called professional site, only to see that it hasn't had any new content added in the last fourteen months or however long? It sends the message that owner of the site doesn't really care about its business or its potential visitors. Show you care by adding new content regularly.

- **Have a blog on your site and write things in it.** One great way to add new content is to post new items to your blog. Do so at least once a week. This doesn't have to be a huge, time-consuming exercise. Even just posting a link to an article or video you enjoyed and you think might be useful for your readers is great. You can certainly do that a few times a week! The point is, if you have people subscribing to your blog, you want to be able to offer them something new often enough that they feel it's worth it, but not so often that you become a spammer. A couple of times a week is enough.

- **Offer something for free.** A great way to entice visitors to your site is to offer a free download of some useful information. Again, this is a great way to position yourself as knowledgeable, while providing genuine value. A great way to extend your network is to offer the information (PDF, e-book, etc.) in exchange for the person's email address to sign up on your mailing list. This way, you can periodically send out emails about new blog posts, or information on additional downloads that your readers will be interested in. An email newsletter doesn't need to be frequent. Even once a month is fine, if you include quality content in it.

- **Let your pages be shareable.** If you have a blog, make it easy for others to share, especially to social media sites. If you can get your readers to recommend your work to others, that's fantastic social proof, and a way of building your reputation. Get enough of those recommendations going, and important people may well begin to seek you out, letting you grow your network even further.

- **Always offer value.** Keep your website simple and relatively brief (you're not a major corporation, after all!), but make sure that everything on it represents you well and offers value. You can include your biography and resume/CV, but it's also great to include testimonials and reviews. You want to show others what you can do for them, not just brag about how great you are (even if it's true!).

- **Always be contactable.** It's crucial that your website make it easy to contact you, in whatever ways you feel most comfortable with. Don't bury your contact page at the bottom of the site; make it prominent and visible. You want people reaching out to you! You may or may not want to put a phone number on the site; a business number might be OK, but don't include your personal number. Instead of your email address (which can invite spam if it's a hot link), use a contact form. This is a great way to keep your email anonymous and still have people reach out to you with ease.

> **"Don't wait until everything is just right. It will never be perfect. There will always be challenges, obstacles, and less than perfect conditions. So what? Get started now. With each step you take, you will grow stronger and stronger, more and more skilled, more and more self-confident, and more and more successful."**
>
> **—MARK VICTOR HANSEN**

CHAPTER 5

CAREER SUCCESS AND PERSONAL SUCCESS

While it's important to be focused on your career, it's equally important to pay attention to yourself. If you are not succeeding in your own life, succeeding at work will be far more difficult. What happens at home will affect your work, and vice versa, so maintaining a stable and satisfying personal life is essential. This chapter will look at some of the ideas about how to approach success in your life and create the conditions that will make it possible, from developing the right mindset for personal success, to keeping a healthy work and life balance, to handling real-life difficulties that can prevent you from achieving your goals.

THE PSYCHOLOGY OF SUCCESS IN YOUR PERSONAL LIFE: EIGHT PIECES OF ADVICE

As we've seen, success obviously doesn't just happen. It's about being active and taking control, but it's also about having the right mindset and way of thinking. This doesn't mean that one has to go into alternative practices, wishing, and manifesting. But it should be fairly obvious that if you think you're going to fail, there's a very good chance that your worries will become a self-fulfilling prophecy. You may even unconsciously put up roadblocks so that if something doesn't work out, you can use that to prove yourself right. This is far more common than you might think, and most people have done it at one time or another. If you are struggling with ideas of how to achieve success in your own life, here are some useful tips for getting around obstacles and getting out of your own way, so that you can start thinking like a successful person before it even happens.

1. **Examine why you are motivated to do what you do.**

   What is it that you want? As in, *really* want? Ask yourself about your short and long-term goals. What's really important to you? What are your main priorities right now? What will they be in a year? Five years? Look at why you act the way you do. Yes, this is a big question and may be too much to take in all at once, but if you can understand some of your underlying motivations, you'll have a better sense of what drives you and of why you value some things and not others. There aren't necessarily right or wrong answers to any of these questions, but it's an important exercise in self-exploration.

2. **Be willing to succeed.** This seems like a strange suggestion, but it's actually obvious when you examine it. If you don't feel you're ready, if you don't feel that you deserve success, whether at work or in your personal life, you may unconsciously find ways to make failure happen. There's no big secret or metaphysical reason for this; it's simple psychology. And it's also important not to blame yourself if things aren't going the way you want them to. Yes, we need to take initiative to make changes happen, but sometimes we get in our own way for reasons that are beyond our control. Trauma, depression, or other mental health issues can all have devastating effects on people's lives and their ability to even cope, much less function, much less succeed. If you are dealing with a mental health concern, be kind and patient with yourself. The Online Resources section (at the back of the book) has some helpful websites. You're not alone, and you deserve a chance to be happy and succeed.

3. **Be open to change.** Nothing ever stays the same, at least not forever. Your life and circumstances will evolve over time, along with your personality, your interests, and your goals. This is not only normal; it's essential. Always ask questions, be curious about things, and be open to being wrong and/or corrected. Admitting you don't know something is wise, and being willing to change directions, attitudes, or actions after learning you were wrong is a key component of future success.

4. **Be concerned with the here and now sometimes.** The past defines us to a certain extent, and it often seems that our entire lives are based around worrying about what tomorrow brings. Of course, if you are success-oriented, you probably have goals, future plans, calendars, to-do-this-week lists, and so on. But the present is the time that exists, and it's the only time you can actually do anything in, even if that is preparing for the future. Be careful about living in the past or future too much, and focus on what you can do right now that will be good for you.

5. **Be grateful.** The simple act of taking stock of what you do have and being thankful for it can be a very reassuring and empowering practice. Some coaches recommend keeping a gratitude journal to write down simple things, anything really, that happens during the day that made you happy, thankful, and so on. Do this for a few weeks and then go back and read everything in there, and you might be astonished at how many good things have happened. It's a great way to remind yourself that the good times often come in these little packages that add up to something much bigger. Keeping track of your small successes will make you feel more worthy and capable of attaining bigger ones.

6. **Visualize what you want.** Again, this is not some magical practice, but merely a suggestion that you get clear, concrete ideas about what it is you want for yourself. And it's not just keeping goals literally in your mind. As with professional aspirations, take the time to write down what you want and need in your life to consider yourself as successful.

7. **Become aware of what you can and cannot change.** There are some things in life that you'll never have control over, mainly to do with others: how they react to you, what they think of you, how they feel, and so on. What you *can* change is how you react to others, how you feel, and how you deal with changes that come your way. It's really the only thing you can control, so letting go of worrying about all of that other nonsense may give you a feeling of peace and being a bit lighter. Once you've set aside others' opinions and actions, you can focus on what's really important: you. You won't have to feel like you are at the whim of outside circumstances, a leaf being blown along by whatever wind comes your way.

8. **Accept setbacks.** As with your professional life, you can't always get what you want. This is most often a temporary bump on the road to success and may mean nothing more than that you have to rethink how you approach a particular goal. Use the disappointment as an opportunity to learn. What can you do to give yourself the best chance of succeeding next time?

PERSONAL SUCCESS IS IMPORTANT TO CAREER SUCCESS

It should go without saying that having a successful real life will help you immensely in your professional life. If you're struggling with personal issues, it absolutely will negatively influence and potentially harm your work. You can't bring your best to the job if personal problems and failures are weighing on you. If you're wondering just how much of an effect your personal life has on your career, here are some examples of how the two are linked, which clearly show that you can't separate the two.

- **Your people skills carry over.** You've been dealing with people all your life, from friends to family to everyone else. If you've managed to find ways of dealing with difficult individuals or resolving conflicts with those that cause you problems (or at least you've come up with ways of avoiding them!), you can bring that ability to work, where you'll likely meet people from very different backgrounds. There will be people that you might not have been friends with if not for your shared work space, and that can be both challenging and exciting. Being open to meeting new kinds of people will enrich your life and give you new perspectives.

- **The quality of your personal relationships carries over.** Studies have shown that people in positive relationships with others, whether significant others or even just friends, will tend to have a better outlook and bring that attitude with them to their work. If you are struggling with personal relationship issues or family problems, it will affect how well you can do your job. This is only logical. If you're upset, or sad, or angry due to personal problems, you won't be able to concentrate as well on your work. It's important that you work to get your personal life in order to the best of your ability and to reach out for extra help when you can't manage it alone.

- **Your time management carries over.** If you're always late for events and meetups, if you never seem to have enough time to get things done, if people are always getting frustrated with how you handle your time, all of this is going to carry over to your job, sorry to say. If you are on top of your time in your personal life, you'll already have the skills you need to succeed with being timely at work. For complete details, see *This Book Will Teach You to Own Your Time*, also in this series.

- **Your dependency on others can factor in.** If you find yourself always depending on others to take care of things, if you rely on them for too much in personal areas of your life, this habit will find its way into your work, and probably not in a good way. The more you can claim your independence in your own life, the more likely you'll be able to work with less supervision and make decisions that need to be made. Being independent and in charge of your life will help you be better at taking charge of your work experience.

- **How you handle money can affect how you work.** You work to get paid, of course, but what you do  with that money can have a big effect on your whole life. Everyone wants to get paid more, but if you're spending too much money on frivolous items, nights out, and other luxuries, it may lead to you taking a very different approach to your work. Your job might become a place of desperation, where you have to go to keep getting the money you need to keep up with your lifestyle. This will likely lead to more stress; maybe you'll start wanting to work longer hours to make more money. But the problem is, those extra hours will cut into your personal time, and then the whole mess becomes a vicious circle. On the other hand, if you manage your money wisely, you can view your work as something that contributes more to your long-term goals. If you feel you are not being paid enough for your work, that's a whole different matter; it may be time to ask for a raise. Bringing this up with your boss can be difficult and awkward, but if you're sure of your value, it's worth considering if you deserve more money.

- **You can get too attached to your work.**
  Maintaining a healthy life/work separation is essential. But sometimes, your work may feel like the one good thing you have, the one thing that you're good at and that you're actually succeeding in. This is a very real and valid feeling, but if you're using only your work as the measure of your success, you're missing a very important part of the whole picture. If the only friends you have are the ones you see at the office every day, it would do you good to expand your social circle a bit more. Don't let your life pass you by because you get so career-focused or work-minded that you neglect those outside of it. It's worth taking the time to develop broader interests and to interact with people that have nothing to do with your employment. Doing so will actually make you a better employee in the long run and will help you fine-tune what your life goals are.

> **"I cannot do everything, but I can do something. I must not fail to do the something that I can do."**
>
> **—HELEN KELLER**

USING OFFICE-RELATED SOCIAL EVENTS TO YOUR ADVANTAGE

Office events can feel like forced fun. If you're cordial but not especially close to your coworkers, having to hang out with them in a social setting might even be annoying if it happens too often. That weekly happy hour or coffee meetup might become a real drag, and you may find yourself looking for excuses to get out of it. But office socials can prove to be quite valuable if you approach them in the right way. Bringing some of your own personality to the event may pay off for you in the long run, because you get to be a bit more of yourself in a more relaxed setting. Here are some advantages to office parties and events.

- **They can improve relations with others.**
  Work environments can be hectic, stressful, and busy, with everyone focused on their tasks to the exclusion of anything else. This may be good for the company, but it can also make employees too focused. The occasional get-together, whether a party, a happy hour, or some  other outing, gives you and everyone a chance to get to know each other a little bit more in a more relaxed setting. Seeing the real people behind the competent professionals can give you a better perspective on the job and help you understand each other better so that you'll work better.

- **You'll feel more like a part of the culture and team.** Having a chance to bond over a drink, laugh a little, or share a story will bring the people in your group together in a positive way and make you all feel like you're a part of something bigger. It encourages the fostering of a unique office culture made up of the unique people in it. Having that sense of belonging will only be helpful for the team as it tackles projects and problems. And having a good feeling about your coworkers will also lessen the stress in the rest of your life. If your job is something you look forward to because of all the cool people there, you'll probably be more happy about your life in general.

- **You have a chance to socialize outside of your usual group.** A larger office or company party may give you the chance to get to know others that you don't work with regularly. This may not seem like a big deal, but as we've seen, from a networking point of view, you might be able to use this social time to make yourself known to others who could be in a position to help you later on. And vice versa, you might be able to offer your services to someone in another department when they need it. This strengthens connections and helps everyone. And you might make a new friend or two!

- **You can use them to practice social skills.** If you're not too comfortable with the whole networking idea, a work social might be a slightly easier place to have a go at it, strange as that may sound. You already have a topic to discuss—your work—and you can stick with a few people from your own group if you're mingling to talk with others you don't know. This can be especially helpful if you're an introvert and don't want to be there to begin with! Small talk about your job will be easy enough, and you can simply move on to someone else when you've had enough.

USING OTHER SOCIAL EVENTS TO YOUR ADVANTAGE

Let's be honest, not everyone wants to be social as much as some do. Studies have shown that a good portion of the population, anywhere between 30 percent and 45 percent (depending on whom you listen to) consider themselves to be introverts. They are quite happy to stay at home, they find crowds and gatherings exhausting, and it's difficult for them to do all the socializing that one is apparently supposed to do to be healthy, happy, and successful. But even the most introverted person will like being around others; it just may need to be in small, quiet situations that the person feels they can control. Regardless of whether you consider yourself to be an introvert or an extrovert, there are ways that social gatherings can be useful.

- **You'll develop a stronger support network.**
  Your network doesn't need to be a lot of people, so whatever your comfort levels are in terms of social interaction, you can create a situation that you're happy with. It's great if there are a few people that you can turn to in times of need or that you can help when they need you; you'll potentially see a tremendous boost in your mood and psychological well-being.

- **Socializing can be good for your health.** Numerous studies show how being around others is good for you. Humans seem to be an innately social species (yes, even introverts!), and we respond well to contact. The Mayo Clinic notes that "adults with strong social support have a reduced risk of many significant health problems," while psychologist Susan Pinker writes that "face-to-face contact releases a whole cascade of neurotransmitters and, like a vaccine, they protect you now, in the present, and well into the future, so . . . shaking hands, giving somebody a high-five is enough to release oxytocin, which increases your level of trust, and it lowers your cortisol levels, so it lowers your stress." So making the effort to be social, even a little, has great benefits for your health!

- **Being more social stimulates our brains.** Studies have shown that our brains benefit from social interactions. People with at least a few regular friends may have better memories and be better protected against degenerative brain problems later in life. An interesting study at UCLA showed that when people learn something in order to teach others (i.e., to be social and interact), they retained the information better than merely learning it to pass a test (i.e., to be analytical and even selfish). Other studies have shown that those with close friends often show greater mental agility in old age.

- **You can socialize as much or as little as you want.** Happily, the health benefits from contact with others do not require massive amounts of time spent around other people (introverts will breathe a sigh of relief!). Any contact is better than none. In fact, most introverts will tell you that they love to socialize one-on-one with someone and may talk for hours about a topic they are interested in. This is fantastic and can produce the same health benefits and psychological sense of wellness. So, whether you want to get out there and go to clubs several nights a week, or stay at home and chat with a friend about the new book you're both reading, you should both be able to reap the benefits of contact.

The point of this advice is simply not to close yourself off and become too isolated. You may be focused on your work, and there's nothing wrong with that, but never neglect the other side of your life, the one you had before taking this job, and that you'll still have after you leave. Having acquaintances at work is fine, but always be sure to give time to your real friends and your family. Try to socialize with them to the best of your ability and comfort level, and you'll see benefits that will carry over into your work.

> **"Trust yourself. Create the kind of self that you will be happy to live with all your life. Make the most of yourself by fanning the tiny, inner sparks of possibility into flames of achievement."**
>
> **—GOLDA MEIR**

SIX ADVANTAGES TO NETWORKING IN YOUR PERSONAL LIFE

Beyond job-related networking, there are always ways of using your personal network to help out yourself and your friends. It should always be a mutual situation, and as with work, you should never only be thinking about what you can get from others. Since so much of networking is about giving, your personal network offers you chances to make connections that would be impossible or at the very least awkward in a work situation; you wouldn't send your boss flowers as a token of appreciation for being your friend. Well, you *might*, but it would probably be seen as a bit weird! And personal contacts might help you in your career in the long run. Again, introverts generally fear and loathe the idea of excessive networking, so we'll include some special advice in the next section for what to do when going out and meeting more people is the last thing you want to do most of the time!

1. **You can help others.** One of the great benefits of knowing more people is being able to help them out in times of need. This isn't about money; it's about having knowledge that might be useful to someone else. If you know a fantastic plumber or the perfect restaurant for a first date, you can give that information to anyone in your network that needs it. This kind of networking is reciprocal. The next time you need a

recommendation for, say, phone repair, it's likely someone in your group will be able to point you to their favorite shop, saving you time, money, and aggravation. Give freely and see what comes back to you!

2. **You'll gain new perspectives.** Knowing different people from different backgrounds is essential to being a well-rounded person. We naturally gravitate toward people that are like us, who share similar views and beliefs, but it's good to get outside your box sometimes and meet people from very different backgrounds. Seeing the world through others' eyes is a valuable life skill that will help you in both your personal and professional lives.

3. **You'll build your confidence.** Forming relationships with others who like you and appreciate you can do wonders for your own confidence. Being around people of like mind and feeling accepted will have you feeling more secure and sure of yourself. This is a valuable attribute to bring in to your work as well. Being able to address others with confidence, state your opinions, and feel grounded will make you a better employee and potentially help your career in the long run.

4. **You may develop lasting friendships.** Most of us only have a few people whom we consider lifelong close friends. Many people will come into our lives for a while, and may be very important at the time, but will then move on and fade away. Expanding your network will certainly allow for more of these kinds of people to join your life, but perhaps you'll meet one or two that outlast that temporary stage and become true lifelong friends. That's always something worth trying for!

5. **It may help you solve problems.** Whatever issue you're dealing with, if you have a strong network of support, you'll be more likely to be able to get assistance when you need it. Having a group of people you trust, even a small one, will leave you not feeling so alone or trapped.

Being OK with relying on others from time to time is a sign of strength, and is another quality that everyone should cultivate.

6. **It might just help your career.** You may not be focusing on your work when expanding your personal network, and, to be honest, you shouldn't be. But personal referrals happen all the time among friends. Maybe you're out having dinner or drinks, and one of your friends happens to mention that her company is looking to fill a new position that is a perfect match for you. With her on your side, you've already got an in and a potential recommendation!

> **"Skill and confidence are an unconquered army."**
>
> **—GEORGE HERBERT**

NETWORKING AS AN INTROVERT: FIVE IMPORTANT POINTS TO REMEMBER

> For introverts, the very idea of reaching out to new people may seem awful. It's bad enough if you have to do it in your professional life, but now you're supposed to do it in your personal one, too?! Joking aside, it can be difficult if all you'd rather do at the end of the workday is go home and curl up by yourself, be quiet, read, watch a bit of television, and undo the overstimulation of the day. Is there any hope for the introvert who wants to network? Happily, yes!

1. **Don't try to be an extrovert.** Just be yourself, and don't feel bad about trying to be more social. Also, don't let anyone berate you over what you're supposed to do. You know who you are, and you're not obligated to change that. Proceed at your own pace and comfort level. You may hate big crowds, and that's fine. Go with what makes you feel comfortable, and don't feel bad about turning down an invite to a big social mixer or party. Many introverts hate parties! At the worst, you may just try going along for an hour or so, and then excusing yourself. Often, it just matters that you made the effort to show up at all. This can be especially true of birthday parties and other gatherings that are deeply personal, which you may want to attend but still find the prospect daunting.

2. **Look for ways to go small.** Big parties suck, but maybe a dinner with three or four people is OK? Maybe getting together with two others for coffee is manageable? You'll know what your tolerance levels are, but starting small is often the best way to go. It may be the most you'll ever feel comfortable with, and that's fine, too. Some of the best social interactions are in small groups (but introverts already know this!).

3. **Look for ways you can initiate socializing that you are comfortable with.** Giving yourself control over the event or gathering will put you much more at ease. Maybe suggest a hike or other outdoor activity with a few others. Maybe a trip to a museum for no more than four people? You can control how many people you'd like to be there, and only invite those that you want to come along and you know would be interested. If you get comfortable with this, it might end up being a regular thing, say, once or twice a month that others really look forward to. Look at you go, you social introvert, you!

4. **Practice meeting new people.** Yes, this may be unappealing, but it's good to try to get outside of your comfort zone once in a while. If the idea of going up to a stranger at an event and doing the small talk thing makes your cringe, change it up. Maybe try talking to someone with one of your friends along, so that there are three of you. If you run out of things to say, your friend can pick up the conversation. Or try asking one of your friends to bring one of their friends that you don't know along for coffee or wine tasting, or whatever. You'll get a chance to meet someone new in a one-on-one situation without the awkward social pressures. In fact, asking for introductions can be a great way to overcome the initial awkwardness and irritation.

5. **Use your experiences to help you.** As you do some of these things more often, you'll likely gain more confidence and may feel better prepared in larger social situations, or even willing to take the initiative and do some networking on your own. No one is trying to turn you into an extrovert, and you don't ever need to be someone you're not. Introverts may be forced to live in an extroverted world, but they can survive and thrive by preparing themselves and taking socializing at their own pace.

> "You miss 100% of the shots you don't take."
>
> —*WAYNE GRETZKY*

EIGHT WAYS TO KEEP A HEALTHY LIFE/ WORK BALANCE

Your work is a part of your life, but it can't be the only thing you do. If it's starting to become that, you need to step back and put up some barriers. It's understandable that you may want to work extra hours and take on more tasks to impress the higher-ups and position yourself for promotion and advancement, but you have to be mindful of your own physical and psychological well-being. No promotion is worth sacrificing your health, your friends, or your family for, and you'll bitterly regret it if you allow work to completely take over your life for too long. Having a life that's separate is essential to keeping your equilibrium. Know when to say no. Here are some tips and observations.

1. **Be prepared to leave work at work.** It really is OK to just let it go until tomorrow. Unless there is some big deadline or crunch time, you'll do far better if you can put work away and focus on other things for the evening. You have to let your batteries recharge, and if you're spending a few hours every night doing extra work, you're not going to be able to do that effectively. Again, unless you are being paid extra for extra work, try to say no when you can. Always value yourself and your worth!

2. **Don't be a perfectionist.** Of course, you want to do your job well, and it's important to take pride in what you do. But be careful about slipping into the trap of obsessing over every little detail such that it slows you down, or requires you, yet again, to take the work home to make sure it meets your exacting standards. Not everything is going to be perfect, and that's also OK. Knowing when good enough is good enough is a sign of wisdom and experience.

3. **Be willing to disconnect.** After a long day of staring at screens, don't spend all night staring at screens. It's important to get away from electronic devices for a while and give your eyes and your mind a rest. Social media will still be there, as obnoxious as always, when you get back to it a few hours later. And definitely leave work chat and updates off! When you're at home, try listening to some of your favorite music, going for a walk, having a good meal, even reading a book for a bit. Do something a bit more tangible and more "analog" than just jumping right into your own emails, social media, and streaming services.

4. **Keep active.** Countless studies have proven the benefits of exercise, so this is probably nothing new to you. But it really is a key part of keeping both your body and your mind in good condition. If you are sitting for long hours every day, it's essential to make the effort to really move at least a few days a week. Humans were meant to be on the move, not be stuck in front of small screens! Having some kind of fitness program (anything from going to the gym, to yoga, to a good walk) will do wonders for your physical and mental state, get the endorphins into you, and improve your mood. Exercise alone if you need to get away from people or make it social if you don't. But keep at it!

5. **Get enough sleep.** Making sure that you have adequate sleep is essential to being able to perform your daily work duties. Don't skip this just because you're young and think you can handle it. There's nothing noble about insomnia or sleep deprivation. Prolonged sleep disruption can lead to serious long-term health problems. Nothing you need to check online is so important that it can't wait until tomorrow; go to bed a little earlier!

6. **Make the time to do something you really enjoy.** Make a list of the things you really enjoy doing or want to do more. Now make a list of some of the things you are doing that are wasting your time (admit it, everyone does them!). Make a commitment to actually trying out some of the things on your enjoy list at the expense of the time-wasters. Do you want to learn a new language? Maybe you enjoy gardening. Even if you can only devote thirty minutes to it at night, three nights a week, indulging in a hobby or passion is a great way to disconnect from work and find yourself again. The mere act of setting aside dedicated time for yourself will also be empowering, if you mark it off and make sure that nothing else can interrupt it. It's taking back control of your own time. For more information and suggestions, see *This Book Will Teach You to Own Your Time*, also in this series.

7. **Take a day off once in a while.** Even if you're not sick, it might be nice to treat yourself to a three-day weekend occasionally. Use that time for something you really enjoy or want to do. Leave work at work on Thursday and don't think about it until you need to go back on Monday. Whether this involves getting out of your town/city for a few days, or just relaxing at home, this kind of mini-vacation can be a great boost if you're feeling overworked or stuck.

8. **When taking a vacation, make the commitment to actually get away.** You've undoubtedly heard stories about CEOs and entrepreneurs who go on "vacation," but spend their time on their phones anyway or read the "most amazing" business book that gives them new ideas for when they come back to the office. Well, good for them. But that's not the purpose of a vacation or downtime. People who are always plugged in never get a chance to rest, and they run a much higher risk of burnout, to say nothing of physical and mental health issues later on. It's OK just to unplug and let work go for a while. Really, it is. And if your job cannot possibly function without you attending to it every day, even when you're away, there is either something wrong with the way your job is structured, or with the way you are approaching it or being asked to approach it. In both cases, this needs to be changed, and you need to think about whether this situation is good for you.

> **"Don't lament so much about how your career is going to turn out. You don't have a career. You have a life. Do the work. Keep the faith. Be true blue."**
>
> **—CHERYL STRAYED**

HANDLING DIFFICULTIES AT YOUR WORKPLACE

You hope that your workplace will be safe, enjoyable, and maybe even fun. You want to get along with people and work together on projects in the hope that a team spirit develops. Unfortunately, this is not always the case. Anywhere that human beings congregate is going to eventually see problems creep in. It's likely that sooner or later, you'll run into some issues of some kind. Here are some of the difficulties you might have to deal with and some steps to take care of them. This is a topic that is far too large to tackle in one short section, but for far more information, see *This Book Will Teach You Business Etiquette*, also in this series.

- **A difficult coworker:** Unfortunately, these kinds of people are almost impossible to avoid. You hope that you'll get along fine with everyone, but there always seems to be that one person that you just don't click with, no matter what. It may be a personality conflict, or it may be something bigger, but dealing with problem coworkers is all too common. You don't want to force a confrontation, and you may even dread doing so, but the longer you let it go, the worse it will get. Try a face-to-face resolution, perhaps mediated by your boss or a qualified third party. Remain calm, don't get angry, and try to see things from their viewpoint (as long as they are willing to do these things for you, too). Talking things through can often clear up the issue.

- **A difficult boss:** This is an even bigger issue than a difficult coworker. You might be able to ignore your coworker most of the time, but if the boss is getting on your nerves (and vice versa), it's a potentially much bigger problem. Speaking directly to your boss about it might be even more difficult. Try to observe if your coworkers are also having problems or if the issue is just with you. It may be that others have complained about the boss' behavior before you. If it seems appropriate, you can speak to HR or someone higher up. If it just seems that your boss is under stress, you may try a direct conversation to resolve the issue. If it's a personal issue between the two of you, mediation may be called for.

- **Sexual harassment:** This is a serious offense, which no one should have to put up with, ever. Your employer is obligated to provide you with a safe and respectful working environment. Sexual harassment can include any number of behaviors: pressure for sexual activity in order to gain a promotion or raise (or not to be fired or passed over for advancement), touching that makes you uncomfortable, someone being too much in your space or following you around, rude comments and remarks or jokes, sending offensive emails, calling you or others condescending names, and so on. If this happens to you or your coworkers, you'll need to decide how to respond in a way you feel comfortable with, but reporting the offense to your boss or HR is usually a good idea.

- **Other inappropriate behavior:** Other obnoxious and unwelcome behaviors may plague your office. These can include gossip; cliques; overly competitive coworkers; busybodies; bullying, derogatory or insulting comments; and anything else that might lead to office turbulence. None of these actions have any place in a professional workplace. Don't engage in them yourself, and if you see them happening—whether to you or to anyone else—take actions to shut them down. Try speaking to the offending party first, and reach out to appropriate authorities (your boss, a higher supervisor, HR, legal, etc.) if the issue can't be resolved that way.

- **Racial bias:** Remember that racial discrimination is illegal. You cannot be asked about your ethnicity or background during a job interview, nor can it ever be an issue when you are on the job. As with sexual harassment, it might take several forms, or it might be a more subtle feeling in the atmosphere of the office itself. How you choose to respond is up to you, but informing your company's HR or other department is a good start. You may also consider checking with your province to file a discrimination complaint. See the Online Resources in the Resources section for more information.

- **Other biases:** Discrimination on the basis of age, sexual orientation, gender identity, religious belief (or lack thereof), First Nations status, and a host of other categories is also illegal and against any reputable company's policy. If you experience any of these problems at your company, refer to your company directives and provincial laws for further help and information. You may wish to speak to your boss and others, and you may be able to file a complaint if the issue is not resolved to your satisfaction. The Online Resources in the Resources portion of the book gives you some good places to begin.

- **Medical and other emergencies:** We all hope that we'll sail through life without any unexpected problems, but this is never the case. In the event that you need to leave work due to a personal or family emergency, your company will probably have policies in place about what you need to do. At the very least, you'll need to inform your boss or manager, especially if you are injured on the job. Your employer is not allowed to refuse your request for emergency leave. Canada has a fairly bewildering array of sick leave laws that vary from province to province, so you'll need to check with yours to figure out what benefits you're entitled to. See the Online Resources in the Resources section for more information.

- **A reminder:** This little book can offer some suggestions and websites for more information, but is not to be taken as a substitute for legal or medical advice. If in doubt, please consult the appropriate qualified professional(s) that you need.

HANDLING DIFFICULTIES IN YOUR PERSONAL LIFE THAT AFFECT YOUR WORK

Life never falls short of tossing us problems to handle, it seems! From day-to-day annoyances to much bigger issues involving finance, health, personal relationships, and dozens of other possibilities, we have to navigate through troubled waters more often than we'd like. And it's entirely possible that some or all of these problems can affect our work; we don't turn those parts of ourselves off at the office. If you are struggling with one or more issues, here is a look at some of the more common problems and how they can interfere with your professional life, as well as some thoughts on what to do to feel more in control and keep them from causing too much trouble.

- **Tell your boss if you're going through a rough time.**
  This may be difficult, but it's an important early step to take, before your job performance starts suffering. Clearly communicate what's happening to you, and assure your employer that you're working through it and will resolve it as quickly as you can. Most people  are reasonable, and your boss may be very concerned about your well-being. They may temporarily assign you less work or put you on a project that is less stressful, so that you can deal with whatever personal matters

you need to. You don't need to go into any more detail than you are comfortable with sharing, and they only need to know how it will affect your work, if at all. If they are courteous and respectful, they won't ask for any more information.

- **Be careful about telling too many coworkers your personal problems.** It may be tempting to reach out to coworkers and tell them what's happening, but be careful and think it through first. Do they really need to know? Possibly, if it's going to affect how you work together, but bear in mind that telling too many people will almost invariably allow for the news to spread even farther. Gossip is, sadly, all too common in places where people gather. Your private life is still private, and you should inform colleagues on a need-to-know basis.

- **Try to compartmentalize your attention.** This can be very difficult, but if you can try to let work be work and your personal life be its own thing, you'll probably be able to handle your work situation better. Yes, that can seem impossible, and it's not something you should beat yourself up over if you can't do it. Think of your work as a way to get your mind off the problem, a chance to distance yourself from it and maybe even get a new perspective. If you are working on specific problems at your job, is there anything in these that could help you in your personal life? If so, give that your attention, and devote yourself to solving the work issue first.

- **Be willing to step back when you need to.** Sometimes, you just need a day or two off. Having a mental health day can be great for clarifying your mind and giving you a chance to rest. Be OK with the idea that you don't just have to plough through work and keep soldiering on. If you've told your boss about the issue, it will probably be fine for you to excuse yourself from work for a day or two. Not being at your best at work does no one any good, so take action to prevent it from happening by giving yourself a break.

- **Reach out to your personal network.** The one place where you can share your concerns is with friends and family. Don't keep things to yourself if you're going through a rough time. You may know someone who has gone through a similar situation, and they might be able to help. Reach out to the right people, not just anyone who will listen.

- **Seek out professional help.** Depending on your problem, you may be seeking out medical help, therapy, counseling, and so on. There is no shame in this; whatever you need to do to feel better and get yourself back to where you want to be is exactly what you need to do. People who see therapists are taking charge of their mental health and working to improve themselves. Just as you wouldn't hesitate to go to a doctor when you were ill (at least we can hope you wouldn't!), feel empowered to seek out whatever kind of help you need.

[

"The greatest difficulties lie where we are not looking for them."

—JOHANN WOLFGANG VON GOETHE

]

HANDLING FEELINGS OF BURNOUT: NINE THOUGHTS

It's possible that at some point, no matter how much you like your job or feel like you're making progress, you'll feel overwhelmed, overworked, tired, disconnected, or at the end of your rope. Maybe you'll just be bored and think, "Is this all there is?" The good news is that these feelings happen to nearly everyone at some point. Being burned out is not unusual, and you shouldn't convince yourself that you're the problem. Understanding the signs of burnout and what to do about them can go a long way to helping you overcome the situation and get back in the saddle again, or maybe point you in a new direction. Here are some of the key signs of burnout (which affect both professional and personal areas of your life), as well as suggestions for how to overcome them.

1. **It's real.** Bear in mind that burnout is a recognized condition, classified by the World Health Organization as a real health issue. They describe it as arising from continual workplace stress that is being ignored or not properly addressed. Over time, this builds up to where you can no longer deal with it or ignore it, and burnout sets in.

2. **There are psychological symptoms.** If you are experiencing burnout, you may feel any of the following: a decrease in interest about your work or even going to your job;

feelings of annoyance, anger, and resentment at the obligations you have; a decrease in the effort you put in; and annoyance at your coworkers or boss, even if they're not doing anything in particular.

3. **There are physical symptoms.** You may feel extra tired, have headaches or body aches, may be losing sleep, or have an upset stomach. Other symptoms include dizziness, chest pain, a tendency to get sick more often, or general feelings of ill health. It's important, if you are experiencing these, to see a doctor and get checked out. You want to rule out any other causes. But if you are basically healthy and you are not experiencing any major problems in your personal life, then you may have to consider that your job is stressing you out to an unhealthy degree.

4. **You need to identify the underlying problems in your life.** If you're facing job burnout, you probably already have some sense of it and what might be causing it. But you may need to dig deeper to look for root causes. Ask yourself if you're being overly hard on yourself or others. Is perfectionism getting you down? Are you constantly feeling inadequate, or that you have to please others? Reviewing your own habits and traits, and how you act on the job, might give you some answers as to why you're taking a downturn. If you are constantly trying to live up to self-imposed standards that you can't meet, it's going to wear you down very quickly.

5. **You need to identify any external problems.** Maybe it isn't you. Are you dealing with extra office stress? Are coworkers causing you problems? Is your boss a bully? If you're finding that your workplace is an unpleasant environment to even be in, it's going to have a huge effect on your ability to get anything done. And if you're facing any kind of harassment, it's going to be even worse.

6. **You need to evaluate your workload.** Maybe you've taken on too much. Even though you're eager to impress and climb the ladder, you may not be able to handle the work you're doing. There's no shame in admitting that you need help or need to share the workload. Talk with your boss about the problem and see if you can get out from under the weight a bit.

7. **Look for some immediate remedies.** In the short term, a few days or a week off from work might be enough to fix the problem, if it's not too serious. If you've been putting off a vacation or even an occasional sick day because you have too much work to do, you need to get over that idea and take the time you've earned. A four-day weekend may give you a fresh perspective and a reset, but it might also reveal that the causes are much deeper and will require more action.

8. **Look at the bigger picture.** How is your job fitting into your longer-term career goals? Maybe you want to stick it out for a few years, with a view toward moving on after that. But if you're suffering now, maybe that's not such a good idea. Are you feeling like your chosen career is no longer such a good fit? Career changes are increasingly common, and your burnout may be related to the fact that you need to make a major transition to something else. It could be the sign you need that now is the time to move on.

9. **Take care of yourself.** Don't just dismiss burnout as having a poor attitude or needing to work yourself harder. Burnout is a genuine health issue that will probably only get worse if you ignore it. Facing up to it may force you into some uncomfortable realizations about your life and career, but it could also be the thing that makes you to take action and move on to a better job, career, and life.

RESOURCES

A short book like this can only explore limited details on each topic, but there is a wealth of information waiting for you out there, if you want to dive deeper into furthering your career development. This section offers both books and online resources to help you in whatever you might need to continue along the path to a successful career.

FURTHER READING

There are many books on career success. Not all of them will be relevant to you, but these titles have been chosen to give you a much broader view of how to succeed, regardless of whether you are just starting out, or have been in the game for a while and want to progress and even start something new.

Christine Brown-Quinn, *Unlock Your Career Success: Knowing the Unwritten Rules Changes Everything* (Rethink Press, 2020).

Mika Brzezinski, *Comeback Careers: Rethink, Refresh, Reinvent Your Success: At 40, 50, and Beyond* (Hachette, 2020).

Jack Canfield, *The Success Principles Workbook: An Action Plan for Getting from Where You Are to Where You Want to Be* (William Morrow Paperbacks, 2020).

Francine Fabricant, *Creating Career Success: A Flexible Plan for the World of Work* (Wadsworth, 2013).

Stephen A. Forte, *Take Off!: 21 High-Flying Secrets for Career Success* (Cloud Nine, 2019).

Marsha Fralick, *College and Career Success* (Kendall Hunt, 2016).

John N. Gardner, *Step by Step to College and Career Success* (Bedford/St. Martin's, 2018).

Dawn Graham, *Switchers: How Smart Professionals Change Careers and Seize Success* (Amacom, 2018).

Sharon E. Jones and Sudheer R. Poluru, *Mastering the Game: Strategies for Career Success* (Drum Major Press, 2018).

Nicholas Lore, *The Pathfinder: How to Choose or Change Your Career for a Lifetime of Satisfaction and Success* (Touchstone, 2012).

Williams McCovey, *Proven Habits for Ultimate Success: Change Your Lifestyle! Fast Success Habits, Best Day-to-Day Practices Development, Upgrade Your Decision-Making Skills & Self-Control for Success* (Independently published, 2020).

Matt Morris, *Goal Setting: 10 Easy Steps to Keep Motivated & Master Your Personal Goals* (Independently published, 2014).

Kathleen G. Nadeau, *The ADHD Guide to Career Success* (Routledge, 2016).

Ray Ralio, *Principles: Life and Work* (Simon & Schuster, 2017).

Dan Schawbel, *Promote Yourself: The New Rules for Career Success* (St. Martin's Griffin, 2014).

Roger Seip, *Train Your Brain for Success: Read Smarter, Remember More, and Break Your Own Records* (John Wiley, 2012).

G. Richard Shell, *Springboard: Launching Your Personal Search for Success* (Portfolio, 2014).

Richard Templar, *The Rules of Work: A Definitive Code for Personal Success* (FT Press, 2010).

Scott Young, *Ultralearning: Seven Strategies for Mastering Hard Skills and Getting Ahead* (Harper Business, 2019).

ONLINE RESOURCES

The following is a list of websites that give more detail on such topics as employee rights, harassment issues, and other legal problems. These are mainly government sites and have extensive amounts of information. These sites will be very helpful if you need further information and assistance dealing with work-related problems. Laws about discrimination and labor rights will vary from province to province, but will not be substantially different than the federal laws listed in some of these links.

Canadian Government: Employment and Social Development Canada

From the website: "Employment and Social Development Canada (ESDC) works to improve the standard of living and quality of life for all Canadians. We do this by promoting a labour force that is highly skilled. We also promote an efficient and inclusive labour market."
canada.ca/en/employment-social-development.html

Canadian Government: Employment Insurance Benefits and Leave

Information on a variety of benefits that you may be eligible for.
canada.ca/en/services/benefits/ei.html

Canadian Government: The Labour Program

From the website: "The Labour Program is responsible for protecting the rights and well-being of both workers and employers in federally regulated workplaces. We work closely with provincial and territorial governments, unions, employers, international partners, and other stakeholders to promote fair, safe and productive workplaces and collaborative workplace relations."
canada.ca/en/employment-social-development/corporate/portfolio/labour.html

Canadian Government: Rights in the Workplace

A resource that includes information and links on the following topics: The Canadian Human Rights Act, The Employment Equity Act, The Canada

Labour Code, Rights for foreign workers, and The Human Rights Maturity Model.

canada.ca/en/canadian-heritage/services/rights-workplace.html

Canadian Government: Sick leave, work-related illness and injury leave, and long-term disability plans

This page offers extensive information on what to do if you need to take time off due to an illness or injury, with a comprehensive FAQ.

canada.ca/en/employment-social-development/services/labour-standards /reports/sick-leave.html

Canadian HRC Equal Employment

From the website: "The Canadian Human Rights Commission conducts audits to determine if employers are meeting their legal obligations to offer equal employment opportunities to four designated groups: women, Indigenous persons, persons with disabilities and members of visible minorities."

chrc-ccdp.gc.ca/eng/content/equal-employment-opportunities-0

Canadian Human Rights Commission

Those who feels that they have been discriminated against can file a complaint, or receive information from this site on how to take their complaint to the appropriate authority.

chrc-ccdp.gc.ca/eng

Public Service Alliance of Canada

The PSAC website offers information on unions and employee rights regarding joining and participating in unions.

psac-ncr.com/union-rights/our-rights-under-law

For more online help with any of the topics covered in this book, a search of the subject you want to read more about should return a good number of results, some of which will go into more detail than a book this size can allow. Many are U.S.-based sites, but the information is generally applicable in Canada, too, unless it deals with specific labor laws and practices.

ABOUT THE AUTHOR

Tim Rayborn is a writer, educator, historian, musician, and researcher, with more than twenty years of professional experience. He is a prolific author, with a number of books and articles to his name, and more on the way. He has written on topics from the academic to the amusing to the appalling, including medieval and modern history, the arts (music, theater, and dance), food and wine, business, social studies, and works for business and government publications. He's also been a ghostwriter for various clients.

Based in the San Francisco Bay Area, Tim lived in England for seven years, studying for an M.A. and Ph.D. at the University of Leeds. He has a strong academic background but enjoys writing for general audiences.

He is also an acclaimed classical and world musician, having appeared on more than forty recordings, and he has toured and performed in the United States, Canada, Europe, North Africa, and Australia over the last twenty-five years. During that time, he has learned much about the business of arts and entertainment, and how to survive and thrive when traveling and working in intense environments.

For more, visit timrayborn.com.

INDEX

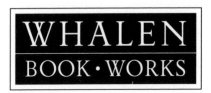

PUBLISHING PRACTICAL & CREATIVE NONFICTION

Whalen Book Works is a small, independent book publishing
company based in Kennebunkport, Maine, that combines
top-notch design, unique formats, and fresh content
to create truly innovative gift books.

Our unconventional approach to bookmaking is a close-knit,
creative, and collaborative process among authors, artists,
designers, editors, and booksellers. We publish a small,
carefully curated list each season, and we take the time
to make each book exactly what it needs to be.

We believe in giving back. That's why we plant one tree
for every ten books sold. Your purchase supports
a tree in the Rocky Mountain National Park.

Get in touch!

Visit us at **WHALENBOOKS.COM**
or write to us at
68 North Street, Kennebunkport, ME 04046

TAKE YOUR CAREER TO THE NEXT LEVEL!